The Anxious Leader

How to Lead in an Uncertain World

by Garath Symonds

Published and Manufactured by Softwood Books
EU Responsible Person: Maddy Glenn
Office 2, Wharfside House, Prentice Road, Stowmarket, Suffolk, IP14 1RD
www.softwoodbooks.com
hello@softwoodbooks.com

EU Rep:
Authorised Rep Compliance Ltd., Ground Floor, 71 Lower Baggot Street, Dublin,
D02 P593, Ireland
www.arccompliance.com
info@arccompliance.com

Paperback ISBN: 978-1-3999-8165-1

"Despite its maddeningly vague, inarticulate form, anxiety is almost always trying to tell you something useful and apposite."

Alain de Botton[1]

A Word on Confidentiality

Throughout this book I refer to my own leadership experience and the work I have done as a coach and consultant, in these examples I have endeavoured to hide the identity of those I worked with to preserve their privacy. The leadership stories I have told are based on real work but are an amalgam of different accounts that try to reflect how we behave when we experience anxiety.

Contents

Foreword

There are moments in every leader's journey when anxiety takes up space between us — unspoken but shaping every move we make. There have certainly been times in my own career, especially as a CEO, when I've unknowingly brought that anxiety into the room — unable to see the cause and effect, or appreciate its impact on colleagues, our culture, and our collective ability to deliver.

Anxiety can't be stripped out of the leadership experience — nor should it be. But our capacity to see it, sit with it, and work with it is what makes all the difference.

I remember the first time I was truly gripped by this idea. Garath Symonds, the book's author, and I have both studied the renowned D10 course at the Tavistock — a place where you learn, often painfully, to look beneath the surface. It's also why I'm so pleased to contribute my reflections here, alongside the valuable insights Garath offers in these pages.

Systems psychodynamics shows us how organisations are shaped by forces we can't always see — the unspoken feelings, group anxieties, and unconscious patterns that drive behaviour. From Wilfred Bion's insights into how groups manage anxiety unconsciously, to Isobel Menzies Lyth's powerful analysis of the 'social defences' we create to avoid uncomfortable feelings, this tradition helps us understand that anxiety is not just an individual burden — it's held and managed collectively. As leaders, the more we can recognise these hidden dynamics, the more choice we have about how to respond. Instead of colluding with defensive patterns that stifle growth, missing opportunities to truly connect, understand problems, and ultimately meet people's real needs, we can contain anxiety, make space for honest conversations, and free our organisations to do their best work.

This is not just an interesting theory; it's an essential leadership skill.

1

And it's never been more needed than right now. Let's face it — we live in wild times. Global conflict, the long tail of a pandemic, seismic shifts towards hybrid and remote work, relentless scrutiny of leaders, and growing levels of disharmony and mistrust in institutions — these are the waters we all swim in. Demand is rising, funding is falling, competition is fiercer than ever, and the social environment feels more volatile by the day. Digital and social media pour petrol on the flames, creating chasms in communities and in people's lives.

In the midst of this, the role of leaders — wherever we are — is to acknowledge and hold these realities while helping our organisations deliver their mission. Emotional intelligence has become non-negotiable, not just a 'nice-to-have.' To be blind to the role of anxiety in organisations is, frankly, to deny its very existence.

I've seen this up close. Years ago, I led a complex merger of two charities. The anxiety for all of us was through the roof. What would this mean for our beneficiaries? How would we integrate two very different cultures? How could we help our people stay on track without becoming overwhelmed by constant change? By leaning in to the anxiety driving behaviours, we were able to have honest conversations — sometimes painful, always real. We focused on our shared assets, rather than falling into the trap of risk aversion, which is the death knell of all meaningful change.

Being anxious is not the end of the world — it's what you do with it that counts.

This is why The Anxious Leader is so timely, so necessary, and, in many ways, so hopeful. Garath Symonds brings more than fifty years of systems psychodynamic theory smack bang into the here and now. He offers leaders a way to understand, contain, and even harness anxiety — transforming it from something that derails us into something that can drive us forward. His models and stories make this deeply relevant and deeply human. I know I will be sharing them with colleagues for years to come. I am so grateful to Garath for the thinking and care he has put into this work — it will help leaders everywhere.

So, if you're ready to look beneath the surface — if you want to lead with more courage, clarity, and care, especially when the stakes are high — you couldn't be in better hands.

"Anxiety is the dizziness of freedom." — Rollo May. May we all have the courage to stand steady when it comes.

Dr Sarah Hughes, CEO Mind UK

Introduction

I never noticed that I was an anxious leader, until events vividly slammed me into this disturbing predicament in a way that made it obvious. It was almost a year after we had been judged as "inadequate" by the government regulator, and I had a new boss. He was one of the cadre of new leaders installed by the Administration in response to our negative judgement. He had replaced my old boss and was going to clean up the mess and turn things around. During our first one-to-one meeting, he never stopped looking at his iPad, reading emails while I introduced myself, and continued to busily swipe the screen. Being deprived of relationship in this subtle and yet obvious way created intense discomfort; I felt ignored and discounted, as if I had little worth. My new boss didn't want to hear about my accomplishments over the last nine years — and my mind was racing to find an explanation for my role in our collective malfunction. When he finally looked up, he described a project that I had led as a central reason for the department's failure and near bankruptcy of the council. Three months later, I was at my leaving party, hosted by the mayor. I left the organisation knowing I had some amazing achievements behind me but, during this project, I wasn't in charge, my anxiety had taken control and steered the ship into the rocks.

It was 2016 and I was in a public-sector leadership role with responsibility for a staff team of over 1,000 people and a revenue budget of over £100 million per year. I was at a career pinnacle of my management responsibility, working in a high-status role within a public body that turned over £1.6 billion each year and served over a million citizens. A few years before, I had led a team that had won a national innovation award, and I subsequently went on to speak nationally and internationally about this project, being seen by some as an expert in public-sector transformation. Looking back, I don't remember being happy or content with my achievements, despite starting out life in a working-class family where men typically drove a taxi for a living. I managed to avoid this and found myself in a team of leaders in the public service, all with very significant responsibilities. I had achieved genuine social mobility and joined a management class that was not accessible to my ancestors.

In this management team, relationships between individuals weren't good. This may be an understatement. A brilliant consultant I worked with at the time described it as "A Game of Thrones". He was right; we were an ambitious group of individuals who showed up at work as if our primary task was to stab each other in the back. This was never said or perhaps even thought, but it was obvious from how we behaved that we believed we were there to fight with our colleagues. Our actual task was to keep children safe; one we were not always in service of, preoccupied with the "Game of Thrones" we were playing.

When I was asked to take over one of my colleague's major projects, I was thrilled. I might have denied this at the time, but I can now see that I felt pleased by her misfortune. My experience of pleasure came from witnessing the failure of my colleague's leadership, an ugly trait I can see in myself, and my hunch is I'm not the only one who can feel like this when they see others fail. On reflection, it was like approval had been withdrawn from the older child and our parent's love had been relocated to me. She had been leading a project to set up a multi-agency contact centre for vulnerable people, in partnership with other public agencies locally. The plan was to build a hub that would be the biggest in the country. After two years of work and many thousands of pounds spent on consultants, the project had made little or maybe even no progress.

For me, the request to take over the project was the public administration equivalent of M assigning a mission to James Bond — I was the hero, the only one who could do the job! The idea that leadership is a heroic activity is one that I had picked up early in life, and had often driven me to act in a way that I can now see was mostly counter to what I was trying to accomplish. At the time, imagining I was a hero helped me tolerate the pressure of the task and step into the role. This simple act of taking up the role of leader created huge anxiety, as the possibility of failure became a vivid and terrifying prospect. To counter this fear, I drew not only on my macho fantasy but also on my own self-belief, and the belief that most senior public sector leaders in the county were putting in me. This faith in my leadership felt supportive and comforting but I also felt alone — as if this was "my" project and not "our" project. I relished the responsibility — feeling special, favoured by those in authority, but I could also sense the peril I was in.

My first task was to write a business case to demonstrate how the new contact centre would reduce demand for services. This proved mathematically impossible, but the head of the council insisted that the target operating model must result in a reduction in demand and, of course, cost. Disappointing my key sponsor felt impossible, so I came up with a hypothecated assumption-laden model that satisfied the project board. That the board accepted the business case was a relief, but it also made me feel a little bit sick. Deep down I knew it couldn't be done, but I was unable to communicate this view in a way that would land. At the same board meeting the head of the police service asked me to bring the project end date forward by three months — his motivation was to get the centre set up in advance of his own inspection of police services by HM Government. This change would mean reducing the systems testing period dramatically. Despite explaining the risks, the change was made, and I began to sense why my predecessor had made so little progress.

Throughout this project I ran on adrenaline, readily supplied by the part of me that thought he was on a 007 mission to save the world. This relentless pace took its toll and one evening, driving home, I found that my mind was not on the road but consumed with the worry of work. I pulled over and began to cry. Despite my upset, a deeply held script written in childhood wouldn't let me give up — I had to achieve to be OK. I wiped my face and called my boss. Explaining how I felt, she gave me the reassurances that I was looking for, and I didn't feel quite as alone as before. Reaching out to people was uncharacteristic of me at the time, and without doing so on that occasion I fear that I would have found myself lost in a dark wood with no easy way out. Ending the call, I finished my drive home, where I opened my laptop and a beer before starting the night shift.

After six months of working at a furious pace, the project was completed on time and within budget, and all that remained was to run the newly established operation. We'd co-located over a hundred staff from council, the police, and the health services; aligning people, process, and technology to improve outcomes for our customers. We felt a huge sense of relief and were determined to make it work. On the go-live day, everything went wrong. The council's internet failed 30 minutes before launch and didn't come back on until the afternoon. We hadn't anticipated this bad luck; I was praying our tech wouldn't fail, never considering the whole infrastructure might have a sick day. By the time systems went back online, we were over a thousand contacts behind, leading to weeks of catch-up. Surprisingly, this crisis management period was less stressful than the change project. However, our IT did fail; the software was inadequately tested and riddled with bugs. We spent a lot of time redesigning business processes and adapting the technology. I felt events were managing me rather than the other way around, and couldn't fathom how this had happened at this stage in my career. We eventually reached a tolerable level of performance after about six months, and I then handed the operation over to the leaders responsible and returned to my day job, relieved it was over but with little sense of achievement.

The impact of this project was considerable. I'm referring to the impact on my body and mental wellbeing. Soon after pulling over my car to weep on the roadside, I found a therapist. Without this support, I would have collapsed into myself, visibly demonstrating an inner world that I was desperate to escape from. We all have our damaged parts; this project activated all of mine. Messages of "you're not good enough" and "work harder" plagued me. The anxiety was relentless, inflicted incessantly as the ordinary background to my organisational life. My determination to succeed created an opposing tension that held me in place long enough to survive. These two forces pulled and pushed in just about equal measure; it felt as if I had forfeited something within me to keep going. When the project ended, I received the validation from the project sponsors that I was looking for, but I was left wondering what had been given up to get it done. A year later and new leadership across the system saw this project differently, questioning what we had done and why we had done it, and I found myself sitting across from my new boss as he scrolled through emails.

Anxiety is an experience felt in the body as a feeling of unease, apprehension, or worry. We've all experienced a feeling of butterflies in the stomach and, at the other end of the scale, being emotionally hijacked to the point of physical and mental paralysis. I've certainly experienced this range, including the times when I've had "performance nerves" that may have helped me succeed. It was on these occasions that my anxiety seemed to energise me towards showing up with greater potency, and I glimpsed how the relationship with this old friend could be different. I saw how anxiety could be experienced as exhilarating — stepping into the unknown felt like a rush. These adrenaline moments were few, and nearly always related to a set piece like an interview or public speaking. Mostly, I thought that anxiety was something to be discarded — it was a problem that needed to be eliminated from experience if I was to be successful in my leadership — a weakness that got in my way. It wasn't until I trained in coaching and consulting at the Tavistock in London that I began to see that it might be my relationship with my emotions that was problematic, and not my emotions at all. That anxiety could be both helpful and unhelpful, depending on how I orientated myself with my experience.

Walking towards the Tavistock Centre for the first time, I passed a statue of Sigmund Freud before entering the concrete and glass building. He peers out boldly, sitting forward in his chair from the corner of Belsize Lane, something like a gargoyle mounted on an ancient cathedral. The place feels half hospital, half university; one gets a sense of an institution with a sense of history and durable convention. The Tavistock has been researching and consulting to organisations for more than half a century, and is world-renowned for its work in understanding organisational life. The Tavistock tradition, also known as the systems-psychodynamic approach, is designed to help leaders make sense of the structure of an organisation — its roles, boundaries, and tasks — as well as an organisation's culture and emotional life. Crucially, the method considers how organisational structure and culture interrelate.

Deeply influenced by this approach, I have come to see how my anxiety was a significant and mostly unconscious influence on my leadership behaviour. Things got worse, however, when I learnt that sometimes my anxiety isn't even mine — it belongs to the group who 'put it into me'! The idea of a group putting their feelings into me was hard to comprehend — it felt like something magical or perhaps mystical. The bad news didn't stop there, as I later uncovered the difficult truth that, as a leader, I not only have to contend with my own anxiety but also that of others. This is no peripheral role of leadership; rather, it is central to the task of leading in a way that genuinely sees and acknowledges other humans. Having spent a career thinking anxiety was a bad thing to be dispensed with, I started to think that it could be an asset that I could use, to track what is happening in me and the organisational system. To do this, understanding what anxiety does to individuals and organisations was essential knowledge.

Viewing anxiety as a prompt for reflection and questioning, rather than something to be treated as we would other ailments, might go against the grain. The dominant idea in organisations and leadership is that anxiety should somehow be replaced with positive thinking and positive emotions

— we should think positively and manifest a better situation. Kindness needs to be instilled where anxiety might invite anger and aggression. In the context of a global mental health pandemic, where anxiety and depression are a menace to the workforce, making space for anxiety seems counter to the prevalent ideas about leadership. This idea may be an even harder sell to the global majority, who face an anxiety-laced stream of racism that runs through so many corporate cultures. Human beings in the 21st century have expressed their identity with greater diversity than ever before, and an industry of equalities, diversity, and inclusion training and consulting has emerged to help protect us against the anxiety of harming others, whether consciously or unconsciously. In this context, we have privileged the importance of so-called compassionate leadership, respect, and kindness as organisations rightly endeavour to avoid bullying and discrimination. In our effort to be kind, something is denied, namely what it is our anxiety is communicating to us.

This book is aimed at those engaged in leadership in organisations, leaders with responsibility for people, in organisations of any size. It draws heavily on systems-psychodynamic thinking and theory about organisational behaviour. I will argue in this book that listening to anxiety's message is not a negation of compassion but rather a promotion of meaning. The hope is that this understanding will help leaders make anxiety an ally, rather than something that blocks their capacity to think and connect with others. It is not an academic text, and I have attempted to use theory to hopefully help locate the ideas in their original foundations. By the end of the book, the reader will understand what anxiety is, where it comes from, and how it can sabotage or aid leadership depending on our relationship to it. Equipped with this understanding, this book offers a practical framework for leading with anxiety — a new call to action.

In the process of telling this story, the links between psychoanalytical approaches to working with anxiety and spiritual practices became increasingly obvious to me. I noticed how psychoanalytical theories relating to the mother-infant relationship overlapped with ancient practices of personal development. In this realisation, the importance of self-leadership emerged as vital to this approach to leadership. However, the journey starts with an exploration of the causes of anxiety, before considering how we defend against anxiety according to the Tavistock tradition. This knowledge aims to help you become more anxiety-aware; to better understand where it comes from and how it shows up in individuals, groups, and entire organisations. In the final chapters, we explore the ways of being that are needed to successfully navigate anxiety before considering the self-leadership necessary to lead in an uncertain world. In this exploration, we make a distinction between being and doing, and consider how our being may be as important in leadership as what we do.

Chapter One

About Anxiety

"Anxiety is the price we pay for being aware of the
complexities of life."

Rollo May[2]

What is Anxiety?

Unlike its cousin fear, anxiety is something without an obvious object of concern. It is nameless and ambiguous and, as such, more dreadful. Our relationship with things beyond the boundary of our understanding — things that are obscured or uncertain — is acutely different from the concrete or simple. Anxiety seems to be a universal experience, common to all humans. It often lurks in the background — sometimes as a low hum, other times as a deafening roar. It is a feeling that often announces itself through the body before the mind can fully grasp its presence. It can feel as though your body is speaking a language of urgency, pulling your attention inward even when you're trying to stay focused on external events. In this sense, it distracts you from what is going on in your external environment and invites you to somehow retreat into yourself.

Forerunners of psychoanalysis in the 20th century, like Sigmund Freud and Melanie Klein[3] both saw anxiety as a fundamental part of human experience, rooted in our earliest years and shaping how we navigate life's challenges. For Freud, anxiety acts like an internal alarm system, alerting

13

us to conflict or danger. It can arise from external threats, but more often, it stems from tensions within — when our desires, values, or fears clash beneath the surface. Freud believed this type of signal anxiety is our mind's way of protecting us, encouraging us to pause and avoid deeper emotional distress. He also traced anxiety back to childhood, linking it to feelings of helplessness when we were completely dependent on caregivers. In adulthood, this can reappear when we face situations that evoke vulnerability, such as high-stakes decisions or interpersonal conflict. The notion of signal anxiety is a central message in this book, a reframing of the anxiety experienced by leaders into data that can inform action and decisions.

For Melanie Klein[4], anxiety begins in infancy, tied to our dependence on caregivers for survival. Klein viewed anxiety as relational at its core, shaped by the bonds we form and the emotional dynamics within them. Far from being merely disruptive, she saw anxiety as a driving force in psychological growth, prompting us to develop mechanisms to manage these fears and navigate our inner world. For Klein, understanding anxiety means recognising its relational nature, and how it connects to our deepest needs for security and connection. Together, Freud and Klein show how anxiety is both personal and relational. It emerges from our internal struggles and our connections with others. For leaders, this means that anxiety is not just a reaction to external pressures but also a signal to reflect on what's happening beneath the surface. Klein developed a concept she called projective identification. This is an unconscious process, although little-known in management circles; it can be found at the root of nearly all organisational dysfunction. Projective identification is a powerful way we communicate — sometimes by offloading difficult emotions onto others, whether intentionally or not. It can be used to hurt, to cope, or even as a way of transforming our inner struggles. Throughout this book, we'll explore the different ways this dynamic plays out in relationships. Once you understand it, you'll have a key to managing your emotions more effectively and leading with greater self-awareness.

Klein identified two fundamental forms of anxiety that shape our inner world and our interactions with others — persecutory and depressive anxiety. Persecutory anxiety is the fear of being harmed, overwhelmed, or attacked — either by external forces or by the projections of our inner conflicts. It can manifest in leadership as the suspicion that others are out to undermine us, or the nagging sense that we are only one mistake away from exposure and failure. Depressive anxiety, in contrast, emerges from the fear that we have harmed others; that our actions — however unintended — may have caused damage. Leaders often carry both, oscillating between self-protection and guilt, defensiveness and responsibility. These anxieties don't just operate internally; they shape relationships, fuelling cycles of blame, withdrawal, or excessive caretaking. Klein saw these tensions as not just psychological burdens but necessary struggles, integral to our growth. For leaders, understanding this means recognising how anxiety can distort perception: the difference between seeing opposition where there is simply challenge, or guilt where there is merely the weight of responsibility. Leadership, then, is not about eliminating anxiety but working with it — developing the capacity to hold both fear and care without being consumed by either.

For existential thinkers, such as Rollo May[5], Søren Kierkegaard[6], and Paul Tillich[7], anxiety is seen as a response to the inherent uncertainties of life. Søren Kierkegaard, often called the father of existentialism, described anxiety as "the dizziness of freedom". He argued that anxiety emerges when we become aware of the vastness of our choices and the weight of responsibility that accompanies them. This awareness can feel disorientating, as we realise that our decisions shape not only our lives but also our identity. For leaders, this can be seen in the anxiety of holding power and authority, the ability to direct teams, organisations, and future strategy, while knowing the outcomes are never fully predictable. Rollo May expanded on this by framing anxiety as a confrontation with potentiality — the realisation that, at any given moment, we face the possibility of growth or stagnation, creativity or destruction. Anxiety, in this sense, is the tension between what is and what could be, a dynamic force that propels us forward even as it unsettles us.

Theologian Paul Tillich[8] introduced the idea of 'ontological anxiety', which he saw as rooted in the human condition itself — our awareness of mortality, freedom, and the absence of ultimate certainty. This anxiety is about the fragility of existence; the fear of non-being and meaninglessness that death evokes. Existential anxiety invites us to face these truths rather than avoid them. It asks us to step into the unknown, to take responsibility for our choices, and to find meaning even amidst uncertainty.

Anxiety, according to some of the key thinkers, is something that can interfere with our leadership, or which has the potential to put us on a path of meaning-making that supports thinking. It makes us do things but also stops us from doing. Both pushing us into action and blocking us from acting. What is vital here is the question: "who has the reins?" Or: "what is my action in service of?" When leading in uncertainty, are you in control or has anxiety taken the reins and control? The answer to this question is not easy because the work of anxiety is nearly always unseen by leaders — in other words, it is unconscious. How we tackle this challenge is considered later in this book, but first the bad news: the context and activity of leadership might just be perfectly designed to make you anxious.

What Causes Anxiety? Our Uncertain World

Organisations today operate in a world filled with uncertainty. What's going to happen economically, politically, socially, and environmentally isn't at all obvious. The news that incessantly streams into our various electronic devices describes a world that is volatile and unpredictable, one where the answer to our global problems is not straightforward, where conflict and chaos can feel normal. In our changing world, technological innovation is explosive, with the potential of artificial intelligence presenting unfathomable sci-fi levels of uncertainty, and climate change making half the planet uninhabitable by the end of this century. In this context organisations operate, and for many, it can feel like a soup of complexity where calamity and catastrophe lurk menacingly around the next corner. It may be that you're not a leader in a global organisation but we are nevertheless all operating in a global context that shapes our everyday reality.

Systems scientist Kurt Lewin[9] calls this wider context 'the field', and it's assumed that "what's out there — gets in here". The thinking is that people and their surroundings and conditions closely depend on each other. In Lewin's words: "to understand or to predict behaviour, the person and his environment have to be considered as one constellation of interdependent factors"[10]. Our context affects us; the uncertainty in the world gets inside us and becomes part of our inner world, influencing how we feel before we even walk through the door at work. Kurt Lewin, in his explanation of field theory, suggests that behaviour is the result of the interaction between an individual and their environment. This theory may help explain how environmental external pressures appear to influence people's behaviour and mindset.

At the time of writing this chapter, political scandals in the UK seemed to be a daily occurrence. Riots were raging across France, and forest fires were scorching the earth as parts of our home became increasingly less habitable for humans. The war in Ukraine was ongoing, as the country with more nuclear weapons than any other continued its illegal expansion project. With no immunity to what happens in the world, supply chains for businesses across the globe were becoming more costly to maintain, and price inflation continued to put businesses, communities, families, and individuals under increasing pressure. My hunch is that by the time this book is published, world events may well seem even more uncertain than they did in the summer of 2023.

I once asked my mother what was happening in her life when she was pregnant with me in 1971-72. She told me the thing she remembered most was the Vietnam War, how she felt constantly upset by the news of what was going on, and how she believed that there could be a nuclear war that would destroy the planet. She was only 19 at the time and I can imagine life feeling very uncertain, carrying the responsibility of a new life inside her. I wondered how this uncertain and anxious backdrop to life affected her and other young people, and how it may have also affected the unborn me.

The term VUCA has been used to try and frame our global context and increasingly that of organisations. It has become something of a management theory cliché, perhaps for good reason, as the idea of a Volatile, Uncertain, Complex, and Ambiguous world clicks with so many business leaders. First used by the US military to describe the 21st-century theatre of war, it has since been adopted by organisational thinkers to reflect the context of contemporary institutions. It's a helpful frame and I wonder if the Vietnam War was any less VUCA than the Gulf War as we neared the end of the century.

When we think about something volatile, we imagine events that change violently and uncontrollably. This was certainly the case during the COVID-19 pandemic, when change was rapid and difficult to adapt to for many, causing significant disruption that was fatal for many businesses, and led to dramatic success for others. The future at this time was uncertain and unpredictable, making it hard to prepare for, and it wasn't easy to see when it would end. This public health crisis made life uncertain and, research shows, created considerable distress for many. Neuropsychologist Tracy Vannorsdall[11], Ph.D., from Johns Hopkins University, describes patterns of anxiety appearing like waves through the population, much like the COVID virus itself. She points to research that supports the idea that a pandemic of anxiety accompanied the virus. COVID was a global-scale encounter with uncertainty that saw a proliferation of worries about our future, perhaps creating a pandemic of anxiety as significant to our health as the virus itself.

Uncertain situations can often involve complexity — lots of moving parts that, when combined with urgency, can create uncertainty that is difficult to bear. The public sector is by no means alone when it comes to having to make sense of complexity, and its context can seem particularly tricky to navigate. The task of many human services organisations can be inherently complex; tasks like reducing crime, improving health, or protecting and educating children, bring social and organisational complexity not as prevalent in organisations tasked with making a profit. This is not to negate the complexity of commercial business, but social problems like crime reduction come with a diversity of root causes that can make your head spin. This is before the various theories of "what works" are considered, along with the patchwork of stakeholder groups, regulatory bodies, the media, public opinion, and the legislative framework. Research evidence suggests that task complexity increases levels of anxiety. Researchers argue that the greater the complexity of a task, the higher the associated anxiety. Complexity can be maddening, creating uncertainty about what to do and where to turn, adding to the sense of being out of control.

If the term VUCA has been relegated to a cliché, it may be because we are getting increasingly used to turmoil as a new normal. Perhaps it always was our normal experience and nothing new? As early as 1971, philosopher Donald Schön[12] commented that:

> "The loss of the stable state means that our society and
> all of its institutions are in a continuing process of trans-
> formation. We cannot expect new stable states that will
> endure even for our lifetimes."

The quote above says more about the world than that other well-known saying that change is normal; it speaks to a vacillating context, where solid ground beneath your feet is rare and the need to adapt to survive is essential. Organisations that operate in this context will have to embrace change

— rather than stability — as a foreground condition. Public institutions that we once relied on to help us feel safe and protected, such as those in the public sector, today seem to be in a state of constant review, economic collapse, reshaping, and crisis. Whether public or private sector, more and more organisations are complaining of being relentlessly busy. With so much going on, things can feel confused and chaotic.

Whether an organisation is operating in a public-, private-, or social sector, our contemporary context can bring forth a real sense of 'not knowing'. This ambiguity experienced may relate to the organisation's key purpose when how to achieve the mission isn't clear. The answer is not simple, and the question "how?" can often elicit a discourse rather than elucidate an obvious way forward. Others may be challenged by questions like how to compete effectively in a reducing market, or how to take costs out when customers are unwilling to tolerate an increased price. Lack of clarity regarding what to do makes for an uncertain world, one where the 'playbook' is no longer relevant; the rules of the game, the players on the field, the ball, and the field itself all seem to be in a state of flux.

The essence of organisational uncertainty is elegantly illustrated by Keith Grint[13] in his description of a 'wicked problem'. According to Grint, a wicked problem is complex rather than complicated; it is intractable, with no straightforward solution, the boundaries of the problem are unclear, and where the problem starts and stops is undefined. Wicked problems are novel, and apparent solutions create new problems. Wicked problems are typified by considerable uncertainty, and require a specific approach to leadership designed to address problems that we've not seen before, that are unknown, uncertain, and where easy answers are unavailable.

When considering the nature of the contemporary organisational context, it may be possible to distil our experience down to one thing: a sense of uncertainty or not knowing.

- We don't know how the system will behave.

- We don't know how to navigate complexity.
- We don't know the answer to the problem.

Not knowing can feel infantilising, taking us back to a child state when we were dependent on the grown-ups for the answers. This is perhaps made worse by the level of expectation we place on so-called leaders. If leaders, like parents, are supposed to know what to do, what happens to the leader (inside) when they don't? Often, a sense of not being up to the job can emerge for them; self-doubt creeps in as they have bought into the expectations of others and feel like imposters. What research shows is that not knowing, or uncertainty, makes us anxious. If this is true, then our context provides an anxious setting for our experience of work before we even attempt to take up our role. It may be that we don't need scientific research to tell us this — if we simply notice our own experience of being in uncertainty, we can verify this supposition for ourselves. The research evidence is there, and we can all relate to the idea that uncertainty makes us anxious; perhaps this sense or experience is the best evidence of all.

Intolerance of Uncertainty

I once described myself at a job interview as "comfortable in uncertainty". Whilst I got the job, I look back on this statement thinking that it conveys a significant lack of self-awareness. That I was never comfortable in uncertainty, but rather, like many successful leaders, I learnt ways of shutting out my feelings that allowed me to get on with the job. It may be the case that tolerating uncertainty doesn't come naturally for many of us. This idea has emerged from research as a primary cause of anxiety, the key component of which was originally seen as a fear of the unknown. Psychologists defined fear of the unknown as "an individual's propensity to experience fear caused by the perceived absence of information at any level of consciousness". According to D.H. Barlow in his 2000 paper in the journal American Psychologist, this fear of the unknown is the basic cognitive process underlying all anxiety disorders. It may be that the human brain was simply not built for uncertainty; it is 'uncertainty averse'. For most of human history we have been hunter-gatherers, living in groups where individuals had established roles and patterns of life. While life could be dangerous for early humans, it was more or less predictable. The brain evolved to be remarkably good at recognising patterns and building habits, turning very complicated sets of behaviours into something we can do automatically.

In 1950 Rollo May wrote:

> "We are no longer prey to tigers and mastodons but to damage to our self-esteem, ostracism by our group, or the threat of losing out in the competitive struggle. The form of anxiety has changed, but the experience remains relatively the same."

From this perspective, tigers and mastodons are viewed as a predictable threat. While they may be life-threatening, they are known, visible threats that can be avoided and tackled through practical steps. In The Meaning of Anxiety (1950), May explains today's threats are to our psychological well-being, and not life and limb. They are, though, uncertain and unpredictable, appearing not from the long grass of the savanna but from shadowy parts of our minds that are out of view. Though sabre-toothed predators are extinct, we conjure them in the form of demanding meetings with volatile managers, peer rivalries, or the ambiguous pressures of organisational life.

In a 2013 paper published in Nature Reviews Neuroscience, authors Dan Grupe and Jack Nitschke[14] focused on the neurobiology of anxiety through the lens of uncertainty, concluding that: "uncertainty results in anxiety". They assert that uncertainty about a possible future threat disrupts our ability to avoid it or to mitigate its negative impact. In other words, feeling anxious about a possible future threat stops us from responding appropriately to that threat. Anxiety can disrupt our ability to think and, therefore, address the very issue that is making us anxious in the first place.

A Leadership Story

The leadership story below captures how external pressures — like market uncertainty and societal challenges — can seep into an organisation and amplify anxiety at every level. It shows how a leader, overwhelmed by complexity and the burden of tough decisions, can become emotionally entangled with the wider context. In this story, we see how easily empathy can give way to frustration when anxiety takes hold, highlighting the challenge leaders face in staying grounded and compassionate when the world around them feels out of control.

What's Out There

Marcus, the managing director of a national environmental services company in the north of England, found himself at a daunting crossroads. The recent loss of several key contracts had triggered a major organisational overhaul, and the board had handed Marcus the unenviable task of reducing the company's headcount by 20%. The country was teetering on the edge of a recession, with a cost-of-living crisis squeezing households nationwide as inflation soared uncontrollably.

Within the walls of the company, a young and passionate workforce thrived. Most of them were fresh out of university, with an average age of just 27. They were driven by a deep commitment to environmental science and sustainability, and for many, this job was their first step towards making a tangible impact on the world. The looming threat of redundancy didn't just spell financial insecurity; it felt like a betrayal of their ideals and dreams.

As Marcus's proposal was unveiled, a wave of anxiety rippled through the company. The prospect of losing their jobs and struggling to pay bills and student loans was daunting enough, but coupled with the relentless news of climate disasters, it felt like the ground was crumbling beneath their feet. The very generation that had grown up with the climate crisis looming large now faced an uncertain future both professionally and personally.

Marcus, in his efforts to engage with his team, was met with palpable fear and distress. The tension was thick in the air — a blend of workplace uncertainty and societal turmoil that seemed impossible to navigate. Initially, Marcus felt a deep empathy for his staff's plight. He understood their fears and shared their anxieties. However, as the pressure mounted, something within him shifted. The constant strain began to wear him down, and a growing frustration replaced his initial compassion. He started to see the younger generation as naïve and overly idealistic, needing to face the world's harsh realities.

This change in Marcus's demeanour seeped into his communications, both verbal and written. His words became sharper, tinged with a bitterness that only heightened the staff's insecurities. What was once a unified team with a shared vision now felt fractured and isolated. The changes were implemented on schedule, but the cost was a deep sense of disillusionment among the employees.

They felt abandoned by a management team that seemed cold and ruthless, far removed from the values that had once inspired them.

***

Marcus succeeds at getting the job done and delivers the cost saving the board had tasked him with. This success came at a cost: multiple sources of anxiety were conflated, affecting staff and seemingly robbing Marcus of his capacity to empathise with his colleagues' predicament, and lead in a way that acknowledged the difficulties they were experiencing. Marcus couldn't tolerate his feelings as he felt the pressure to get the job done, and he resisted thinking about what might be needed. Anxiety stopped him from thinking and reflecting — vital capacities for leadership. Instead, he resorted to action, knowing that doing stuff would make him feel better and keep the board happy

Early Anxieties

From a psychoanalytical viewpoint, our capacity to tolerate uncertainty and anxiety is significantly influenced by our early childhood experience and how we were supported to relate to uncertainty as an infant. The skill of processing and making sense of anxiety is learnt early, and can shape our relationship with anxiety into adulthood. On those occasions when we experience situations that are in some way like early past events, our internal voices can become stimulated. I was recently coaching a CEO from the health sector who seemed disproportionately upset by the partnership she was working in, which was seemingly turning a blind eye to a significant risk. It looked like this was repeated by a series of different agencies in the partnership, to avoid one very powerful stakeholder from taking responsibility for the financial implications of this risk. When we dug into her experience, we discovered a link to a family dynamic where the behaviour of a powerful family member was continually covered up since her early childhood, to protect him from taking responsibility for his inaction. Once again part of a dysfunctional system, now in adulthood, this situation activated her unconscious resentment and anger when the group turned a blind eye to what was really going on.

Figures from the past, often authority figures now internalised, can pipe up — and often in a way that is not helpful. These voices can mobilise early parental reprimands that can be frightening because they reside deep within us. They can survey us from an inner vantage point, holding us to account for failings we hide from everyone else. Larry Hirschhorn, in his book The Workplace Within, described these messages as "voices that shame us in front of ourselves alone"[15]. It is as if we revisit childhood experiences, transported by boardroom friction, a difficult conversation with the boss, or project disappointment, to infantile memories and a level of development we had thought we had surpassed. Perhaps Marcus, in our story above, was tormented by these internalised authority figures, shaming him in front of himself alone. He felt an overwhelming pressure to deliver the change regardless of the loss of goodwill that it caused.

Decisions and Tasks Cause Anxiety

Even when authorised by the system, decision making, for example, is always a rendezvous with uncertainty. Making a decision requires us to commit to an uncertain future. It also means cutting away the other options. Both this commitment to an unknown path and the loss of other possibilities can cause anxiety. This anxiety is often related to the quality of information available on which to base the decision, and it shows up throughout the process, lingering as you wait and see what the decision's consequences are. This may help explain the thirst for information and analysis that we see in modern organisations, as companies continually search for greater insight into the market, workforce, and their context. We can find comfort in an analytical report that tells us what is going on, and gladly pay the consultant who provided it as certainty increases and our anxiety recedes.

Perhaps all organisational tasks carry something uncertain — will we succeed or fail? This potential failure holds the possibility of letting down authority figures who reside in our inner world. These figures move about the world with us and are based on our earliest experience of authority — our parents, or those who took that role in our lives. We then transfer the characteristics of these figures onto external figures in authority, evoking an infantile reaction to authority, which almost inevitably makes us anxious. Sometimes the task itself is a source of anxiety. Imagine what it would feel like to work in a cancer unit where death is a normal part of the job, or a team that is working to tackle child abuse. Increasingly, calls to a customer service helpline include a recording that says, "Please be kind to our staff" before the call begins. These messages always remind me of the potential anger of customers that those who staff these helplines may have to contend with. These tasks evoke anxiety that can be overwhelming, limiting our effectiveness at work.

We Imagine Threats That Aren't There

Mark Twain is often credited with saying, "I'm an old man now and have had many problems. Most of them never happened." It's a sentiment that resonates with many of us, the mind's ability to conjure problems that don't actually exist. Dr Hannah Rose explores this unconscious tendency to anticipate negative outcomes and to assume that they are more likely than positive ones. This habit of giving credence to imagined scenarios can obscure clear thinking, distorting decision-making and potentially imped-ing progress. We catastrophise and think the worst, driving up our anxiety levels. Rose goes on to describe our fear of loss. Research has discovered that a structure in the brain called the amygdala is more sensitive to loss when anxiety is present. This sensitivity may lead us to make a decision that seems to be less likely to lead to loss, even when our assumptions are not always based on reality but an imagined catastrophe. This process of imagining future negative outcomes is also reflected in psychoanalytical thinking, as we deny reality and invest our attention in fantasy that keeps us attached to the status quo. Our current situation may well be sub-optimal or perhaps even awful, but it is known; it is connected to certainty in a way that the future is not, and we say, "Better the devil you know…" The problem with the "devil we know" is that he seeks to keep us just where we are, stuck in an organisation that fears letting go of the known, as its context transforms and leaves it behind.

This is seen in the sometimes radical change experienced when trying to keep pace with technological progress, or when we try to meet changes in market demands. The effects of change can be made better or worse depending on an organisation's ability to protect itself and its staff in response. Or, in other words, how well we prepare staff to let go of the "devil we know" and then relate to the "the devil we don't". From a sys-tems-psychodynamic perspective, one key way of supporting staff during change is structurally; this relates to the boundaries of an organisation — its task — the roles people take up, and the nature of organisational authority. Levels of anxiety in organisations are directly linked to these structural factors and significantly influence how well the organisation is set up to hold people's anxiety: the policy framework of an organisation that tells staff how to behave; the organisational structure that shows us our relationships to others; the job descriptions that define our role and responsibility; the mission statement that tells where we are going. These all help in the task of managing anxiety and their absence or ambiguity can cause anxiety.

This means that whenever we change the boundaries of our organisation, roles, and leadership structure, we invite the opportunity for anxiety to creep or perhaps flood in. Change is an inherently uncertain business. As we cross the threshold from something that is known into what is unknown — a new market, a new organisational structure, a new business process, a new technology — all represent significant changes creating uncertainty that have an emotional impact on people in organisations. The absence of organisational structure in the form of clearly defined teams, roles, policy plans, and processes causes anxiety as we feel untethered from something certain, something that helps us make meaning of our task, role, and place in the organisation.

Anxiety is Contagious

A key challenge presented by anxiety in organisations, which can show up very obviously at times of change, is that it is contagious — perhaps even viral — in how it can spread and infect an entire system. Psychoanalyst and organisational consultant Deirdre Moylan[16] warns of the dangers of contagion in her contribution to the 2019 book Unconscious at Work. Moylan describes how our feelings can be communicated unconsciously and non-verbally through a process known as projective identification (more on this idea later). In this way, feelings from one person are attributed to another. We've all noticed how someone else's emotional state can affect us or how the boss's worry can make us feel worried. Psychoanalytical thinkers also believe this happens more subtly in ways we don't notice. Feelings that are not ours can be put into us, and we feel what someone else is feeling. Before too long, a feeling like anxiety can be spread around a group as we unconsciously share our feelings with others. Larry Hirschhorn[17] talks about 'the anxiety chain', a chain reaction where one person's anxiety triggers another and can be passed around like a common cold. In this way, we might take anxiety from one meeting into the next, contaminating the room without noticing, and we go on to infect others. Like Rose, Hirschhorn goes on to describe how we invent or imagine fantasies that help us deny the reality of what is happening — those events that are causing the anxiety. This fantasy is more palatable than what is really going on and we invest our energy into it, as questioning it would be connecting with something too difficult to think about.

Anxiety at the Boundary

Perhaps the most uncertain and anxiety-provoking place to be is on the edge of things — the place where there is less safety, where you risk slipping and falling into the unknown. We sometimes talk of "being on solid ground" and we know what that feels like; it's reassuring and gives us confidence. Whereas being on the edge entertains the possibility of mishap in a way that solid ground does not. We may experience this boundary organisationally on the dividing line between teams, the line that separates them and us, or as the boundary between the organisation and its market, its customers, and competitors. All are perhaps venues for rivalry, uncertainty, and the possibility of winning and losing. We can also create boundaries between us and those we see as different, so-called others who don't share our identity or experience. In this case, not letting the other in, in case they harm us. We can see this boundary being defended in prejudices and bias — how we discriminate against people because of perceived differences that are seen as somehow intolerable.

These boundaries can be both structural and psychological; the agoraphobic may feel safe sheltered by the walls of their home, as what's unsafe lives beyond those walls, beyond that boundary. Similarly, our organisation or team may provide a sense of safety or shelter, where venturing out into the wider organisation or the environment external to the organisation represents risk. The sense of belonging that so many managers endeavour to cultivate can help provide teams with a sense of safety, but it can establish a so-called 'silo' inhibiting collaboration and cooperation, keeping people inside unable to leave the safety of the team. Leadership is an activity that happens on the boundary, mediating what comes into the organisation and what is exported into the external environment. Without leaders managing a boundary, teams and organisations are open to being invaded from the outside, or are not sufficiently held together to feel safe enough to get work done. Imagine being in a team where requests for work come directly from a powerful authority figure, like the CEO of the company. You have your regular work plan but the CEO shows up demanding more, in a way that it feels impossible to say no to. This can feel overwhelming to staff, and lead to sense of burn out. What's missing is the management of the boundary, your boss gatekeeping what comes in and out of the system, 'managing up' and regulating the CEO's demands directly with them.

Uncontained

Tavistock pioneer Wilfred Bion, who founded the psychoanalytical study of group life, developed the idea of 'the container and contained', that helps explain this relationship we have with boundaries. Bion, who was a First World War tank commander, saw our need for containment expressed by British Army Tankies' affectionate name for their weapon: Mother. Consciously or unconsciously, members of the Tank Corps saw a link between being in the safety of their mothers' womb and being in an armoured container on the battlefield. Both represent a place of relative safety, and a boundary between some certainty and some significant uncertainty. Perhaps we remain in our little tanks from infancy, whereby we armour ourselves against the uncertainty of the outside world. The boundary represents the dividing line where certainty ends and uncertainty begins and, as such, at some level remains terrifying.

Bion, crucially, linked his idea of 'container-contained' to our capacity to think. Bion's idea of the 'container' was that it functions as a place where we locate emotions like anxiety. Anxiety can overwhelm the container, impeding our ability to process and transform raw emotional data into thoughts. When the container fails to function properly, thinking becomes blocked or distorted. With our container full of anxiety, we are left without the capacity to hold our emotions, and the result is we can't think. Ignoring your emotions by somehow denying or avoiding reality may not help, instead resulting in a whack-a-mole situation where your emotions splurge out in an uncontrolled manner. Lack of containment causes anxiety — when we don't feel safe or contained, nothing is stopping the unknown terrors from an outside getting in. In these circumstances we adapt, and endeavour to defend ourselves from anxiety, lest it destroy us. It is these adaptions or defences that we will explore in more detail in the following chapter.

Leaders Create Anxiety

A mentor once said to me, "as a leader you are always being watched". At the time, this felt like helpful feedback, as I noticed how my mood and body language had an impact on the people around me. It's perhaps obvious that a leader's communication, verbal and non-verbal, will affect followers for better or worse. What's perhaps less obvious is that we might be unconsciously communicating our feelings to others regardless of what we say, even how we say it. According to psychoanalytical theory and specifically an idea called projective identification (that we will explore in the next chapter), emotions are being subtly relayed to others all the time. If we feel anxious, then this will be picked up as an unconscious communication despite any rhetoric saying the opposite. Equally, we are continually scanning our environment for threats. As Rollo May reminds us, threat is no longer from wild predators but to our self-esteem and sense of safety. As leaders, it is then vital that we remain mindful about what we might be communicating, and remember that our followers' anxiety detector is always on.

The idea that we are an emotional beacon that broadcasts a signal all the time, even despite our verbal and physical communication, might be hard to grasp. If true, this idea introduces a new perspective on emotional regulation. Namely, that the difficult task of not openly expressing your emotions is only part of the challenge — that there is a need to transform your emotions because they will be expressed unconsciously without your conscious involvement. In this sense, leaders become a source of anxiety, as their inner world is communicated to the system. What leaders represent in systems means that this communication is amplified, and the impact is more significant than for those without a direct leadership role. This doesn't mean don't feel, it means reflecting on and processing your feelings, as an individual and with other people. This task is central to becoming an anxiety-aware leader, and how to do it is considered throughout this book.

Key Takeaways

1. **Anxiety as a Universal Experience:** anxiety arises from uncertainty and manifests physically and emotionally, often before the mind fully comprehends it. It signals both internal conflict and external pressures.

2. **Perspectives on Anxiety:** Freud viewed anxiety as an internal alarm rooted in early helplessness, while Klein[18] emphasised its relational nature, shaped by dependency and fear. Existential thinkers linked anxiety to freedom, mortality, and responsibility, framing it as an unavoidable human condition.

3. **Leadership and Uncertainty:** leaders often face ambiguous and high-stakes situations, resulting in anxiety linked to a lack of clarity, heightened responsibility, and fears of inadequacy.

4. **Emotional Contagion:** anxiety is not confined to the individual; it spreads through organisations via unconscious processes like projective identification, where feelings are transferred between people, influencing group behaviour.

5. **Anxiety as a Leadership Tool:** when embraced and reflected upon, anxiety can enhance awareness and inform thoughtful leadership. When ignored, it can block critical thinking, fuelling defensive behaviours such as blame and avoidance.

Chapter Two

How We Defend Against Anxiety

"We would rather be ruined than changed. We would rather die in our dread than climb the cross of the present and let our illusions die."

W.H. Auden[19]

Follow the Anxiety

In the 1976 film All the President's Men, the screenwriter William Goldman attributed the phrase "follow the money" to Deep Throat, the Washington Post informant who took part in uncovering the Watergate scandal[20]. The phrase is not mentioned in the non-fiction book that preceded the movie. However, the book does include the phrase: "The key was the secret campaign cash, and it should all be traced"[21]. Understanding how you defend against anxiety and, therefore, how you avoid the pain of facing reality, can help leaders see what is going on in their systems. Whether within yourself, with groups, and whole organisations, this involves following the anxiety to its source, to find out what is causing the presenting dynamic and how might we address the situation, in doing so we need to 'follow the anxiety'.

How We Defend Against Anxiety

According to Sigmund Freud, the pleasure principle is a fundamental organising force of the human psyche. It drives individuals to seek pleasurable experiences and avoid discomfort or pain. Perhaps it's no surprise then that when we experience anxiety, we seek to rid ourselves of it. We have, in fact, designed a variety of ways of doing this very thing, most of which provide us with at least some temporary relief from this seemingly pernicious human experience. This pattern of behaviour may be a big problem for leaders, since it may be counter to their task: that of mobilising people to achieve a common goal. And organisational life and leadership (as described in Chapter One) might be inherently anxiety-provoking.

When we can't tolerate our anxiety, it is said to be "defended against"; we refuse to engage with or consciously appreciate what we are feeling and seek to rid ourselves of this unwelcome experience. The process of unconsciously trying to get rid of our unwelcome feelings is reckoned in psychodynamic theory to be an early (or "primitive") defence; this means it starts in infancy. When we resist any conscious appreciation of our anxieties, we deny the reality of what is taking place. In doing so, we exclude vital data about our predicament. Perhaps worse still, we create dysfunctional relationships with others that erode our capacity to collaborate and think creatively as a team.

By understanding how these defences work, leaders can develop a deeper awareness of how anxiety influences behaviour — both their own and that of their teams. This awareness is crucial in recognising when defences are taking over, and learning how to address anxiety in ways that foster growth, connection, and resilience. Through stories, theory, and practical insights, this chapter aims to help you see anxiety not as something to be eliminated but as a force to be understood and navigated. In doing so, you can move from an unconscious reaction to intentional leadership, using anxiety as a guide, rather than a barrier, to meaning-making and connection with others.

A Leadership Story

The leadership story below explores how one leader's personal anxiety subtly but powerfully shaped her behaviour. It's something many of us can relate to — those moments when the fear of being challenged or exposed makes us build barriers, often without realising it. This story highlights how a leader's need to protect themselves from uncomfortable feelings can inadvertently create distance and frustration in their team, showing just how much anxiety can have an impact on relationships and collaboration.

Kept at Bay

Emma, a vice president at a large retail company, had a well-known habit that had slowly begun to erode the fabric of her team's sense of belonging: she simply couldn't stop talking. Whenever meetings were held, Emma dominated the conversation, her voice an unending stream that left no room for others to contribute. Her colleagues found themselves increasingly frustrated, feeling as if every attempt to enter the discussion was met with swift interruption. To them, it was as if Emma was deliberately "keeping us at bay", maintaining a tight grip on the dialogue and leaving no space for alternative viewpoints.

The team's reactions to Emma's overbearing behaviour varied widely. One colleague, weary of the constant interruptions, adopted a stance of resignation. "OK, go on then, Emma, you tell us…" he would say, waving his hand in defeat, allowing her monologue to continue unchecked. The fight to interject had long since drained him of the energy to confront her relentless flow of words.

Another team member took a different approach.

Determined to be heard, he mirrored Emma's behaviour, speaking rapidly and without pause, forcing his points into the conversation before being inevitably shut down. It became a battle of wills, a chaotic clash of voices vying for dominance in a space where true dialogue was almost impossible. Most found themselves becoming very passive, withdrawing and resigning themselves to the fact that Emma didn't want to hear what they had to say.

Unable to be heard, the team felt unvalued and excluded; it was as if the purpose of conversations with Emma was to sit passively and be talked at, or fight her to get a word in edgeways. The team was left frustrated by this dynamic but could also see Emma was a good person, who was often capable of kindness, and someone who advocated for the team across the organisation. They were unable to communicate the impact her leadership style was having, fearing that it might hurt her; it was this that kept them stuck.

***

The expression "kept at bay" comes from the 14th century, when barking dogs were kept from attacking; tethered to a post, they were unable to harm passersby. Could it be that Emma saw the views of her team as attacks? And that these attacks needed to be kept at bay to avoid being bitten by a raging dog? Perhaps what was being attacked was her sense of herself as a leader; a fantasy of omnipotence, of needing to be right or a desire to be heard? The idea of a different perspective was too difficult for Emma, evoking a sense of being out of control, and she defended against the anxiety of this threat by putting a wall of words between her and the individuals in her team. It was as if the bad ideas existed in the team, and she had to protect the good ideas by keeping her colleagues out of the conversation.

In this example, Emma was seemingly unable to tolerate the possibility of different views in case they inferred she was somehow inadequate, and she defended against this anxiety by creating a barrier of words, cemented with her positional power, to keep the alternative perspectives out. This behaviour was temporarily effective in relieving anxiety but left Emma with a residual feeling of disconnect; an unconsidered knowing that something wasn't quite right, a feeling she pushed out of her awareness, protecting her from being exposed to what was really going on. In this way, she was able to keep her feelings at bay, denying her experience; she worked to build a wall or psychological boundary to protect herself and keep the threat out. Conversely, the fear of hurting Emma's feelings by communicating her impact kept the team from having a potentially difficult but reparative conversation.

Once again, the team were kept at bay by anxiety; this time it was the fear of harming someone that blocked them from exercising their personal authority and talking to Emma.

***

Individual Defences

This tendency to deny our feelings, rather than think and talk about what is going on, may have its roots in infancy. Melanie Klein[22] worked out that in infancy, we defend against anxiety through a process she called projective identification. Think of a baby who feels the pain of hunger for the first time; she has no understanding of what this pain is and even believes that she will be destroyed by it. Her instinct is to get rid of these feelings, which she does by an unconscious interaction with her mother or main caregiver. Her feelings are experienced by the mother as if they were her own. Notice how a distressed baby can make the mother feel distressed. In this way, the preverbal baby is relieving herself of difficult feelings and communicating something to the mother.

What has this to do with leadership, you might well ask? Projective identification doesn't stop in childhood; whilst first observed in infants, the process continues into adulthood when we experience situations that evoke unwelcome feelings. In fact, it's going on all the time, and it is a primary way we defend ourselves against the anxiety of living an organisational life; moreover, it's a key way we sabotage collaboration and productivity in organisations. The psychological mechanism discovered by Klein[23] in 1946 is central to the Tavistock approach of organisational consulting, and may be at the heart of all organisational dysfunction. It is, though, a somewhat technical concept that isn't easy to grasp — leading it to be excluded from the mainstream leadership development agenda.

It may be helpful to think of projective identification as something we have imagined; an idea where we unconsciously attribute something about ourselves to another. Often, it is something we find we don't like about ourselves; a so-called "bad" part. We see that badness in the other and deny its existence in ourselves. This is called 'splitting', and is followed by projection; we hold on to our "goodness" and locate the bad bit in the other. We then treat the other as if they contain the "badness"; we treat them as if they are bad. A clue to when this is happening is when we feel overly hurt, defensive, or sensitive about something someone has said or done; when we are highly reactive and quick to blame, and find it hard to be objective and put ourselves in the other's shoes. The other can then enact, or act out, the feelings they experience as if they were feelings that belonged to them alone. When what is happening is that the other's feelings are being communicated to us via a projective process and we assume, in the absence of reflection, that they are our feelings. The reverse can also happen, where we attribute competence or confidence to someone else and are unable to see the part of ourselves that has these qualities. This is called idealisation, and we see it when we put leaders on a pedestal and make them idols, discounting our own capacities.

The process of projective identification typically follows the steps below:

1. **Experience:** An emotion is experienced.
2. **Denial:** This emotion is too difficult to think about and is denied or resisted.
3. **Splitting:** A psychological splitting occurs into "good" and "bad" parts.
4. **Projection:** The good or bad feelings are projected by attributing them to another (person or group).
5. **Relief:** This provides temporary relief for the projector and communicates their feelings to the receiver of the projection.

It is helpful to understand how projective identification works at the level of an individual, but the psychoanalytical view of how organisations function regards the individual's unconscious process as subsidiary to what is going on within the wider system. The anxiety-aware leader may be better served by thinking more organisationally or systemically; learning to reflect on what the organisation is doing to activate the behaviour in the individual. More about how this process works at a group and an organisational level later.

A Leadership Story

This leadership story is about how a leader's inner struggles with self-doubt and fear of failure can play out in their interactions with others. It's an all-too-familiar scenario: feeling overwhelmed, we shift the focus away from our own discomfort and onto others. In this case, it's blame — used as an unconscious defence against the anxiety of feeling inadequate. This story invites us to reflect on how our own defences can ripple outward, affecting not just ourselves but also the people we lead.

The Blame Game: Part One

Jon was a newly appointed vice president in a global pharmaceutical company, where he was leading a particularly challenging project. The project wasn't going well, and Jon felt out of his depth, unable to make the impact he desired with this, his first time leading a major project. He felt anxious and out of control. These feelings evoked the idea that "I'm not up to the job". Reflecting on where these feelings might have come from or what they might mean was too painful for him and he resisted this reflection. In this way, his feelings were denied. Jon also failed to consider other data, including his previous track record of success, that might counter this idea that he was not up to the job; he was unable to see both.

Jon felt not good enough, but rather than own these feelings, he unconsciously looked for somewhere to put them where he didn't have to deal with them. This process prompted the idea that "I'm OK, it's not me, it's my team — they are the problem." He was saved by the notion that he was not to blame; it was someone else's fault. This felt right to Jon, relieving him of the guilt of his poor performance and offering him salvation. As a result of this realisation, he became overly critical, harsh, and abrupt in how he related to his team. The team began to feel incompetent and blamed.

The project manager who reported to Jon was called Simon; he was very experienced and had been in the company for over a decade. As the project slipped, deadlines were missed, and budgets overspent, Simon felt increasingly unsupported and under pressure. This feeling tipped into a sense of being overwhelmed at a project board, where the anger of senior sponsors, including Jon, was openly expressed. Simon's project highlight report was criticised and rejected in a way that felt personal and shaming. The following week, Simon left the organisation. After a brief conversation with an HR adviser, he was asked to collect his things and leave.

***

In the days after Simon left the organisation, the feeling in the team was that he had been unfairly blamed for project failures that were shared by the team and which were also a consequence of a very challenging context. Rather than take a measured look at what was going on, the project board found it easier to pin it all on Simon and, in doing so, save the VP from the damning judgement of his peers. This process seemed to have begun with Jon's failure to take responsibility for his feelings of inadequacy. Unable to reflect on his experience, he attributed his unwanted feelings into his team. When discussing what had happened, the team felt that Simon had been scapegoated by the organisation. One colleague said: "Making Simon the scapegoat doesn't solve the problem; the board have blamed an individual and have not seen how difficult this project is."

The idea of the scapegoat is recognisable to many, and illustrates the process of projective identification that can take place when someone is singled out to take the blame. We scapegoat as a way of avoiding blame or taking responsibility when it's too difficult to own. The term's origin is biblical; the concept first appears in the Book of Leviticus in the Old Testament; the Israelites conduct a ceremony in which they direct their sins onto an escape goat. The goat is then set free into the wilderness to cleanse the wickedness from their community. The goat then bears the burden of taking on the misdeeds of a tribe. Like the scapegoat concept, this magical thinking has us believing that the problems of the organisation or project, in this case, can be discarded if we attribute them to an individual and then exclude the individual and the problems from the boundary of the organisation.

In this example, it was as if the board were designated for the task of selecting the 'escape goat' and they put the group's sins into Simon, casting him out into the wilderness and cleansing the project of its failures. Projective identification is central to the process of blaming; it involves people denying the totality of what is going on and attributing their difficult feelings to an individual or group. The scapegoat is an image we understand, an ancient story that reflects how the tribe can attribute its unwanted thoughts and feelings to a chosen target and, in doing so, seemingly relieve themselves of any responsibility for what has taken place.

This process might be familiar to those who have worked in organisations trying to "turn around". On those occasions that an organisation is judged to be going in the wrong direction, turnaround leadership is often called for. Something goes wrong, there's a major failing; perhaps a review or investigation to work out what happened takes place first. The board appoints a new leader, a hero from a foreign land charged with saving the organisation. This new leader starts his turnaround of the company's performance by removing the old leadership, making them the escape goat, then casts them out into the wilderness along with the company's woes. Doing this can make the new leader appear strong and decisive, and perhaps discounts the real story behind the headlines and the capabilities of the people being removed. There are, of course, occasions when there is a good case for changing leadership, and even when organisations have had a clear out at the top, they can find themselves frustrated when organisational patterns and behaviours don't change.

***

Group Defences

Wilfred Bion suggested that all groups have an unconscious desire to find leadership, and that this is determined by the group's belief about "who or what will save us from the mess?" A very visible idea is the notion of the turnaround manager described above; someone explicitly tasked with cleaning up. Bion saw the necessity of group development and how this involved growing pains that needed to be worked through. This development requires groups to work to understand how unconscious processes, like projective identification, might be getting in the way of their effectiveness and preventing them from achieving their objectives. Bion saw this development work in groups as vital in helping the group see the reality of their situation and think about what to do. He noticed that this developmental work is often avoided in groups as it's difficult for us to own our stuff and be vulnerable, especially in front of others. The desire to find leadership persists and leads groups to a trio of unconscious assumptions that allow us to keep going. He called these assumptions 'basic assumptions', and the groups that are influenced by them 'basic groups'.

Bion put forward the following three basic assumptions that groups unconsciously make to help them deny reality and the pain of development:

1.   They assume that the group has been brought together to fight or flee from an enemy (Fight/Flight).
2.   They believe the group is dependent on a powerful leader (Dependency).
3.   Or they think they need to oversee the marriage of a pair who will produce a leader or solution (Pairing).

As indicated, these basic assumptions are called 'fight/flight', 'dependency', and 'pairing'. They can be spotted when groups behave "as if"; as if they are to fight or flee from a common enemy, as if they are dependent on a powerful leader who will come with a magical solution to their problem, or as if a pair will in some way give birth to a solution that will make things better. Organisational consultant Jon Stokes called the 'pairing' basic assumption hope, as we put our hopes in the pair's potential to solve the problem, to provide leadership. All these assumptions characterise the ways teams work as an alternative to accepting the reality of their operating context and cooperating.

The main feature of basic assumption behaviour is the speed and ease with which the group take up and display these assumptions. They don't go through a process of group development; rather, they unconsciously collude to create a group culture or climate that plays out the assumption. This all happens outside of conscious awareness, and Bion argues the behaviour is centrally related to feelings of anxiety. Bion believed that facing our anxiety requires developmental work at a personal and group level. We resist this often-painful work of taking responsibility for our "stuff", opting rather to hold onto the fantasy that leadership will come from something external to ourselves. In this way, we collude with other group members and avoid the difficult developmental work needed to complete the task.

Yet groups are not always trapped in basic assumption thinking. Bion contrasted this with the 'work group' mentality — a state in which a group faces reality, acknowledges its purpose, and cooperates to achieve its task. A work group does not surrender to unconscious fantasies about rescue but instead tolerates uncertainty and the discomfort of thinking. It works with creativity and discipline, navigating differences without resorting to blame or magical solutions. Unlike a basic assumption group, which clings to defensive postures to avoid anxiety, a work group can tolerate the reality of their experience and treat it as something to be understood rather than fled from. The challenge for leaders is not just to manage teams but to help them stay in 'work group' mode, resisting the seductive pull of basic assumptions that promise relief but ultimately derail progress.

A Leadership Story

The Meeting gives us a glimpse into how anxiety can quietly take over a group, steering it away from real collaboration and problem solving. It's something we've probably all experienced — those meetings that feel like they're going nowhere, where people talk around the real issues, or where tensions bubble up but never quite get addressed. This story shows how a group's shared anxiety can shape the way they interact, creating behaviours that might feel like progress on the surface but actually keep them stuck. It's a relatable example of how our unconscious defences can show up in even the most routine parts of organisational life.

The Meeting

The meeting started late as usual. The chair dispensed with introductions despite some new faces around the table and got stuck into a very crammed agenda, remarking: "We've got a lot to get through; best make a start." For the first 20 minutes, Sally from marketing noticed the chair did most of the talking. He seemed unable to discern any progress on actions from the minutes and ploughed on, tackling the agenda at pace. By now, Sally was feeling the urgency in the room and the desire to get through what felt like an impossibly large list of things to discuss. The quarterly performance data was introduced by the head of business insight. As she began, colleagues around the room started complaining about the quality of the data, spelling mistakes in the slide deck, and other minor inaccuracies. The company's insight team became a target for the group's anger, and the issues behind the declining sales were not considered. At this point, Sally felt a mix of panic in the face of the aggression and boredom being expressed. This was the way we did things; it had become expected and normal. As the chair laboured through the performance slides, he occasionally stopped to ask questions and request comments. Contributions from others weren't forthcoming, and the chair filled the empty space with his analysis, to everyone in the room's relief.

In the second half of the meeting, the FD presented a financial report. This was not well received, evoking anger from several operational directors, claiming inadequate support from Finance. At this point, two operations directors started discussing the specific difficulties in their areas. This seemed to Sally to be a very local issue, and she felt somehow excluded from the conversation. It was as if they were having a conversation amongst themselves that everyone was spectating. In the last 10 minutes of the meeting, Sally noticed how many people were checking emails, eyes flicking across their screens indicating their absence. Others had their cameras off and were invisible. She felt relieved she wasn't called on to speak as the chair thanked everyone for another productive meeting and closed proceedings 13 minutes late.

***

Perhaps the meeting was highly productive, if we think about the real purpose of the meeting. Could it be that the meeting's unconscious purpose was to avoid the task of leadership? In this respect, it was very successful. The meeting started typically late, perhaps suggesting a desire not to be there and a flight from the task before the meeting even began. The agenda

filled to the brim with items of business may indicate a busy organisation, and perhaps one that seeks to avoid its tasks by failing to prioritise.
Crammed agendas are easily explained by the volume of work in the business, and it may indicate that the group is feeling overwhelmed by the task
and denies it by making it overtly undoable.

The chair ignored the new faces, disassociating from people; he made
some members of the group literally nameless and as such easier to ignore.
He then forced the agenda through as if to say, "I know the answers – you
can rely on me". Bion's basic assumptions seem to show up in this example
in the way the group flees from its task, looks to the powerful leader to
take control, and in how they made a common enemy out of the insight
team. With the performance slide deck, the focus on spellings and minor
mistakes could indicate a corporate commitment to excellent standards or
perhaps a desire to avoid a real conversation about performance, where
a fight with the people who produced the data felt more attractive. The
dialogue with the two operations directors appears to be a pairing that the
group unconsciously assumes will magically solve a problem, enabling
them to do all the work on the group's behalf. The lived experience in the
room was of feeling excluded from a dyadic recital of a two-way conversation. The conversation was not about the poor financial performance
that the directors were responsible for but rather the quality of the support
offered by the Finance team; again, relatedness was dodged, and so was
a real conversation about the issue at hand. Avoiding relating to people
is a helpful way of staying at the surface level and not seeing the other's
human experience. This allows us to deny what might be happening and
avoid exposure to something difficult.

Online and hybrid meetings can often offer various ways of avoiding
the difficult, and not really showing up. It's easy to work out when someone is 'multi-tasking', checking email and other tasks, their eyes flicking
from keyboard to a screen with the video minimised at the periphery of
the screen. When cameras are turned off, that sends a different message,

one that implies a physical removal from the conversation. The behaviours seen in The Meeting reflect an organisation stuck in a basic assumption mentality, seeking to fight or flee from the task or find leadership in a powerful leader or a pair who will provide hope. These behaviours are always to defend against anxiety. It doesn't mean that nothing ever gets done; sometimes you get lucky. What it means is that work is off-task. The group is not working creatively and cooperatively to achieve a task that they all understand; it is instead unconsciously colluding to avoid the reality of their context and the pain of development necessary to work effectively. This development would involve being vulnerable, sharing their real feelings in a way that connects them to others and their task.

Spotting when basic assumption behaviour is at play can be an art, and we can probably all discern what it feels like to be on-task, in your flow, and making progress as opposed to being engaged in activities that feel avoidant and tense. Meetings are often a great place to be on the lookout for off-task behaviour that conveys that something other than cooperation to get the job done is going on. As mentioned earlier, when the group is cooperating and thinking creatively towards a goal that they all understand, Bion called this a work group. Neither the work group nor the basic group are permanent states but rather modes that groups move in and out of. The trick is noticing what mode you're in — either basic- or work-group mentality at any one time.

***

Social Defences

First developed by Elliott Jaques and Isabel Menzies Lyth[24], social defence theory looks at how an individual's psychic defences interplay with an organisation's defences. Social defences serve as bridges over the turbulent waters of anxiety, but when too fortified, they keep us from confronting the reality of the river itself. This was clearly highlighted by the groundbreaking research by Menzies Lyth into nursing practices in a British teaching hospital. The research uncovered how patients and their relatives made psychological demands on the nurses that increased the nurses' experience of stress. Nurses had projected into them feelings such as depression, anxiety, and fear by patients and their relatives so that they would experience these difficult feelings instead of (or partly instead of) themselves. In doing so, they also communicated their experience to the people they felt dependent upon for help. Social groups in any organisation can use these defences. The ten defences described below may be familiar, and they were all described by Menzies Lyth in her seminal research.

10 Defences Against Anxiety

1. Splitting of Roles

Helplines that require customers to speak to multiple representatives for a single issue often illustrate the defence of splitting. Each representative handles a specific piece of the problem, ensuring no one is fully responsible for its resolution. This structure reduces the anxiety of bearing the full weight of a complex issue, fragmenting responsibility across the system. While this protects staff from the emotional burden of accountability, it can leave customers feeling more anxious and frustrated as their concerns are shuffled between departments. The system prioritises managing the organisation's anxiety over providing a seamless service to the customer.

2. Depersonalisation

In schools, the use of formal titles such as "Mr," "Mrs," or "Ms" among teachers, even in private conversations, demonstrates depersonalisation. This practice creates a sense of distance and formality that can shield teachers from the emotional weight of personal connections in a high-stress profession. By depersonalising colleagues, parents, or management, teachers avoid recognising their shared vulnerabilities and emotional realities, easing the pressures of interpersonal dynamics. Similarly, broader organisational labels like "management" can dehumanise those in leadership roles, reducing the anxiety of addressing them as individuals while sustaining an "us versus them" dynamic.

3. Detachment

Legal professionals and accountants who consciously avoid empathising too deeply with their clients exemplify detachment. This defence allows them to maintain professional boundaries and avoid becoming overwhelmed by their clients' struggles. For example, a lawyer who adopts a formal and distant manner during meetings might be protecting themselves from the emotional toll of their client's distressing situation. While detachment can help maintain professionalism, it may also distance workers from the reality of the issues they are meant to address, limiting their effectiveness.

4. Ritualisation

Organisational consultations with staff or customers often take on a ritualistic quality, where the process is followed meticulously but the substance is ignored. For example, a company might conduct a lengthy consultation with employees about a new policy, only to proceed with its original plan regardless of feedback. The ritual of consultation provides a container for collective anxiety, allowing leaders to claim they've listened while avoiding the discomfort of engaging with the real concerns and emotions of those involved.

5. Dissipating Decision Making

In heavily regulated industries, decision-making processes often involve excessive layers of approval and rechecking, ostensibly to ensure accuracy but frequently to avoid committing to a course of action. For instance, in some organisations, proposals can circulate endlessly between departments for sign-off, each layer acting as a shield against the anxiety of taking responsibility. While these processes can be justified as governance, they often leave organisations paralysed, avoiding risk and progress.

6. Ambiguity

Ambiguity arises when organisational roles, tasks, or policies are deliberately left unclear, creating confusion that allows anxiety to dissipate. For example, in a company with undefined team responsibilities, staff may spend time debating who should take ownership of a task rather than addressing it. This confusion can act as a policy for inactivity, enabling the organisation to avoid confronting challenging realities or making difficult decisions.

7. Distorted Delegation

In some organisations, junior staff are overly dependent on senior leaders, attributing all competence and authority to them while avoiding their own responsibilities. Conversely, senior staff may delegate excessively, avoiding their high-level responsibilities by occupying themselves with tasks suited to junior colleagues. For example, in a consultancy firm, partners might insist on reviewing every minor detail of a presentation, sidelining junior staff, and avoiding the strategic work only they can perform. This mutual collusion protects both levels of staff from the anxiety of fully owning their roles but leaves the organisation underperforming.

8. Resisting Change

Resistance to change often stems from a collective fear of losing established social defences. For example, in a manufacturing company, employees might resist adopting automation not only because of potential job losses but also because the current manual systems represent familiar routines that contain anxiety. As automation threatens to dismantle these routines, it provokes heightened anxiety, leading to resistance that delays necessary transformation.

9. Putting It Off

Recruitment processes are often drawn out unnecessarily to avoid the anxiety of hiring decisions. For instance, a company might repeatedly extend the interview process, claiming it hasn't found the "right fit". In reality, the position may symbolise unresolved organisational dilemmas, such as replacing a well-loved leader or addressing structural weaknesses. By never finalising the hire, the organisation avoids confronting these deeper issues, keeping the vacancy open as a form of defence.

10. Avoidance

Risk management processes can sometimes serve more to manage anxiety than actual risks. For instance, a risk register that spans hundreds of pages and requires lengthy review meetings may provide the illusion of control without genuinely mitigating critical threats. The detailed documentation and process act as a defence, containing collective anxiety about uncertainty while preventing focused discussions on the most pressing risks. By focusing on the process rather than outcomes, the organisation avoids engaging with the full reality of its vulnerabilities.

These examples illustrate how whole social groups can unconsciously collude in a way that is off-task but allows the group to avoid facing something difficult. All organisations employ social defences; often these can be helpful and assist in coping with anxiety in an on-task manner. For example, how those in blue-light services like social workers, firefighters, or police officers use dark humour to disassociate from the anxiety of a task that brings them into contact with human tragedy. More often, social defences help to avoid a reality, and the development needed to face it, in a way that is dysfunctional and off-task.

A Leadership Story

In the leadership story below, we return to Jon, vice president in a global pharmaceutical company. The story developed when Jon employed a consultant to help him think about what might be happening in the system. It was then that Jon discovered that blame was used as a social defence against anxiety across the systems, and how he had potentially been pulled into an unconscious process that was playing out organisationally.

The Blame Game: Part Two

Struggling with feelings of anxiety and guilt, Jon could feel something wasn't right. Whilst it felt obvious to him to blame his team for the challenges with his troubled project, he also felt unsettled and agitated, particularly by Simon's abrupt exit. He held on tightly to the idea that the issues with the project were an incompetent staff group's fault but at the same time, knew there was more to the story than he could discern. He felt stuck and confused. Not being able to explain these feelings, he looked to an external consultant for help. The consultant worked with Jon for several months and was able to help Jon see that blame was central to his work system. The company had formidable corporate governance arrangements in place to scrutinise clinical, financial, and managerial practice. The notion of accountability was a central value, and this translated to a practice of blaming individuals and groups for failings in the system that were inevitably a collective responsibility.

On continued examination of the culture with his consultant, it became clear to Jon that a 'blame game' was playing out as routine organisational activity. It had become normal and difficult to notice. Jon went as far to say that "it was as if our purpose here was to avoid blame." This showed up in group emails that were experienced as persecutory and shaming, pushing the recipient into defending themselves and trying to evade culpability. Blaming people not in the room or not present in a meeting was normal and staff colluded with this practice, relieved it wasn't them taking the blame. The term "thrown under the bus" was a part of the corporate lexicon that portrayed a culture that prized survival. People would both complain about being "thrown under the bus" and at the same time joke about "throwing someone under the bus".

The culture of blaming instigated an industry of back-covering activity that went beyond normal good governance. Staff would go out of their way to cover their backs with emails and audit files that kept them out of the bus lane. In a moment of depressing revelation, Jon suggested that "99% of our energy goes into avoiding blame, and 1% for our actual job." Later, he concluded that: "It's probably why we're all so exhausted, having to do the job with so little energy left to spare for the task."

Another common expression was "air cover".Colleagues would often ask: "Do you have air cover?", meaning "have you sufficiently covered your back?" The expression comes from warfare and refers to the use of aircraft to provide aerial protection for ground forces against enemy attack. In this sense, the blame game was weaponised, requiring air support for those on the ground. The picture held in the organisation's mind was clearly of being at war. By reflecting on this culture, Jon could imagine that he had been unconsciously recruited by the system to express blame on its behalf. In doing so, he discounted his team's ability to fix its problems and denied his part in the poor performance.

***

In the example above, the activity of blaming others and avoiding being blamed was used as a defence against anxiety across a social ssystem (organisation). The possibility of being publicly shamed and judged as a failure by the system created considerable anxiety, that people fought against by blaming others or fleeing from by covering their backs. Both these activities are a retreat from the organisation's primary task in service of an unconscious or perhaps unsaid alternative primary task. This task could be inferred by how people behaved, an "as if" task. It was as if this system was exquisitely designed to get the results it was currently getting, both structurally through its corporate governance arrangements and also the culture of blame and persecution that accompanied this structure.

One result of this functioning is that decision making becomes difficult and laboured, as leaders, teams, and committees are reluctant to take responsibility for something they could later be blamed for if it went wrong. An industry of bureaucracy and administration had consumed decision-making processes in Jon's company, making the task of decision making almost impossible. Deciding puts us in contact with uncertainty and therefore anxiety, as we consider the possibility of making the "wrong" decision. In cultures in which there are high levels of blame, the fear associated with making decisions becomes a major obstacle to progress, promoting the idea that "nothing gets done around here". Ultimately, the threat of being "thrown under the bus" and the effort to "secure air cover" was exhausting, and preventing the organisation from making progress.

Anxiety is an inevitable part of leadership, but its impact is shaped by how leaders engage with it — whether they react defensively or approach it with awareness. Defensive patterns — both personal and organisational — often emerge as automatic responses to uncertainty, manifesting in avoidance, control, perfectionism, or scapegoating. Left unexamined, these defences can limit perspectives, reinforce silos, and undermine trust. By recognising, following, and reflecting on these patterns, leaders create the conditions for greater psychological openness — both within themselves and their teams. This awareness is not about immediate resolution but about staying present to what is unfolding, allowing for more thoughtful, intentional leadership. In environments where anxiety is acknowledged rather than suppressed, leaders can cultivate cultures of adaptability and shared responsibility, enabling their organisations to navigate complexity with greater resilience.

Key Takeaways

1. **Defences as Coping Mechanisms:** in response to anxiety, individuals unconsciously develop defences to protect themselves from discomfort. These defences, such as denial, projection, and avoidance, may provide temporary relief but can obstruct meaningful engagement with reality.

2. **Impact of Individual Defences on Leadership:** leaders may overcompensate, blame, or dominate conversations as unconscious ways of managing their anxiety. This behaviour can alienate teams and disrupt collaboration, reinforcing the very issues the leader is trying to avoid.

3. **Projective Identification:** a key psychodynamic concept, projective identification involves unconsciously attributing difficult emotions to others, who may then start to feel and act out these projected feelings. This process often underlies workplace conflicts and dysfunctional team dynamics.

4. **Group Defences and Basic Assumptions:** groups also develop shared defences against anxiety, such as dependence on a "saviour" leader, avoidance of difficult tasks, or projecting blame onto others. These basic assumptions can derail the group from its core objectives.

5. **Navigating Anxiety-Conscious Leadership:** by recognising and reflecting on their own and their organisation's defensive patterns, leaders can move from reactive to intentional leadership, fostering openness, collaboration, and resilience in the face of uncertainty.

Chapter Three

Leading With Anxiety

*"Let everything happen to you: beauty and
terror. Just keep going. No feeling is final."*

Rainer Maria Rilke[25]

When we lead with anxiety rather than fight against it, we open ourselves to a deeper understanding of our emotions. An anxiety-aware leader sees anxiety not as something to fear but as a signal — a form of intelligence that can guide thoughtful leadership. Instead of being swept away by anxious feelings, you can pause, contain the emotion, and ask yourself: what is this anxiety trying to tell me? Developing this skill helps you steady yourself during challenging moments, making space for clearer thinking. Once you can contain your emotions, you're better equipped to help others navigate theirs, transforming their overwhelming feelings into something more manageable and constructive.

Stories can be particularly powerful here. Think about leaders you admire, or perhaps moments in your own journey when you witnessed someone steady the room during difficult moments. These stories remind us that leading with anxiety isn't about perfection — it's about finding calm amidst the storm and also showing others that this is possible. In this chapter, we'll walk you through three key steps in the aware-leader method — a practical process designed to reshape your relationship with anxiety and enhance your self-awareness as a leader. You'll also learn why creating organisational structures that provide containment, including reflective spaces for your team, is essential. These spaces offer a way for anxiety to be acknowledged, explored, and worked through — fostering a calmer, more resilient workplace. As you read, consider how stories — both your own and those you encounter — serve as tools for reflection, bringing the abstract concepts of observation, containment, reflection, and awareness to life.

The Pause, Think, Act Method

The pause, think, act method empowers you to lead with anxiety in a way that dramatically shifts your relationship with this seemingly maleficent emotion. It provides you with a template to transform anxious feelings experienced as an individual leader, those of groups, and your entire organisation. Whilst the diagram below illustrates this model as a three-step process, everything happens at once. It is a holistic way of being that starts with a pause.

Figure One: The Method

1. Pause

The first step in the process actually involves three little steps all taken at once, and it's called a pause. What actually happens is you pause, notice, and contain. Three interconnected moves are described here as one conscious action.

In a rapidly moving organisational context, it's easy to get caught in the relentless cycle of reacting to demands, solving problems, and making decisions. Yet, in the midst of life a simple practice can make all the difference. To pause is to step to one side of your mental and emotional train and intentionally create a space to breathe. It's a deliberate interruption of the automatic, reactive patterns that so often dominate our days. In this pause, we allow ourselves to tune into what is happening — within us, around us, or between us and others. Noticing is what follows, as something suffused with the pause. It's a moment of curiosity, a quiet attentiveness to the present. Perhaps you notice the tension in your shoulders, the tightness in your chest, or the shallow rhythm of your breath — all signs that anxiety is present. Or maybe you observe a dynamic in the room, an unspoken tension between colleagues, or the energy shift after a challenging question. This act of noticing, done with openness and without judgement, creates a window of awareness. And in that awareness lies choice.

The capacity to pause and simply notice may well be transformational, not just to your leadership but to your development as a human being (more on this in the final chapter). Despite this, we potentially spend most of our waking hours asleep, not noticing what is taking place in our experience. The first step in becoming a more aware leader requires you to wake up to what is happening in your experience. Simply notice that you are feeling anxious and acknowledge your emotions. This may sound easy but as we've already learned in Chapter Two, we devote a huge amount of energy denying and avoiding our reality.

By moving away from the experience of anxiety, we move away from the reality of our experience and miss an opportunity to understand what is taking place. To notice requires you to be present in your body. When we have uncomfortable feelings, our tendency is to distract ourselves. The invitation here is to do the opposite and go towards the discomfort. This means placing your attention on your body, sensing your physical body, and fully experiencing the feeling of anxiety. This action accepts your experience and is a voluntary decision to suffer your anxiety without any effort to push it away. The original meaning of suffer comes from the Latin sufferre, meaning "to bear under" — not just enduring pain, but allowing something to happen. To suffer, in this older sense, is to permit, to make space for, to tolerate — even when what we allow may bring discomfort or uncertainty. The box in this chapter describes how it works in practice.

By pausing and noticing your experience in the manner described above, the process of containment begins. When we pause, something is held; we suspend the need to reflexively react, and we instead hold ourselves. The task in this step is to contain your experience, to create a barrier between the turmoil and disruption you are feeling inside and your reaction to this. Often, anxiety can provoke a reflex action in us, we might lash out, panic, express anger, or become aggressive. We often say things we later regret, or it may elicit a more passive response as we cower from our feelings. Reflexively reacting to anxiety can destroy leadership, as followers learn to fear a leader's reaction or lack confidence in their passivity. By containing anxiety, we create an inner vessel in which to locate it and hold it in.

Pausing: imagine a surge of anxiety entering your body. Against all your instincts you focus your attention on your breath and bodily sensations, and in doing so invite the unwelcome feeling in. Your breath and bodily sensations act as a handrail that allows you to stay upright despite this unwanted invasion of emotion. You do not judge what you are experiencing, good or bad, you simply become aware of it, how it feels, its texture and quality, whilst at the same time staying connected to your breath and your body. This is your experience, your reality, you do not push it away — you sit with it and experience your anxiety fully.

By refusing to identify with or become our experience, we make material available for examination. It is no longer something I am enmeshed in and is rather an object that I can observe and make sense of. This process may require what Daniel Goleman[26] called emotional intelligence: "the capacity for recognising our own feelings and those of others, for motivating ourselves, and for managing emotions well in ourselves and our relationships"[27]. In his classic text Emotional Intelligence: Why it can matter more than IQ, Goleman initiated a self-help revolution, helping millions of readers develop what he called emotional literacy or EQ. He encouraged working on yourself as a leader to improve emotional regulation, avoid being hijacked by your emotions, and improve your relationship with yourself.

Creating this inner container is an exercise in emotional intelligence or regulation, as you locate your anxiety in a space ready for the next step. It is also a space created by leaders that can be used by followers. Followers put their anxiety into the leader through the process of projective identification described in the last chapter. The leadership task is to treat others' anxiety in the way described above — to pause, notice, and contain it. Not only does this make the anxiety available for thinking, but it also modifies it through a process called reverie.

Reverie is the ingredient required to modify the others' emotions; this is something that a leader does for followers. We will explore this idea in greater depth later but for now it may help to think of it as a form of compassion, where one suffers alongside another and thereby changes the experience of suffering. It requires the leader to adopt a calm and receptive state of being that contains the others' anxiety and enables the conditions for change. Individuals can use the same process as they employ self-compassion and "experience their experience" as if they were alongside themselves. This somewhat esoteric practice is covered in Chapter Six.

> **Containing**: the effort to contain your anxiety without outward show is an inner struggle. It means holding yourself together to avoid any ruptures or leaks of emotion that might be expressed in an unregulated way, verbally or physically. It involves creating a holding environment inside that can also be used by others. As a leader, you are required to contain yourself and provide a container for the emotions of others. This is achieved through finding a calm and receptive state of being; like the skill of noticing, the foundation for this capacity is present-attention, awareness of your breath and bodily sensation. Feeling the energetic vibration of your body allows you to ground yourself, to locate yourself in the here and now, where you can simply notice and contain your experience in your body.

2. Think

A leader's capacity to think perhaps represents their most valuable asset, but thinking is so often obscured by anxiety. Anxiety and the associated defences we establish to contend with our difficult feelings prevent us from seeing things as they really are; all too often we can create a less threatening fantasy to invest our attention in and avoid the pain of reality. The return on this investment is not good, as it inevitably results in actions that are not grounded in your operating context (your experience). Real thinking, as opposed to reflexive reactions designed to defend against anxiety, is founded on a sense of containment. The leader is required to create this sense of safety for themselves and for others. From this place of safety, it is possible to find a place in your mind from where you can observe what is taking place; not as someone overwhelmed by their difficult emotions, but as an objective third party, an impartial witness of events. The lens through which events are observed is curiosity and questioning, the task is to learn about yourself and the system in which you are working.

Our ability to reflect on our experiences, especially during times of pressure, is significantly supported by what British psychoanalyst Ronald Britton[28] referred to as 'the third position'. This concept also has its roots in early childhood and the dynamics of our relationships with our parents. Britton proposed that if a child can mentally accept the reality that their parents share a relationship independent of the child, a new relational perspective emerges — one where the child becomes an observer, rather than a participant in that relationship. By adopting this third position, the child gains the capacity to observe the parental relationship and to imagine themselves being observed in return. This development enables a person to step into the perspective of the other — to see the other's point of view, put themselves in the other's place, and also observe themselves. Britton[29] described this third position as "a place in my mind that I could step into sideways from which I could look at things." For leaders, this vantage point offers a crucial means to make sense of their circumstances and realign themselves with their emotional experience. The problem is that anxiety can take us back to an earlier stage of development and get in the way of more mature responses.

Thinking requires containment, a sense of being held and supported. Leaders may find this exteriorly in structures, like their role and position, as well as in the support of others, but ultimately, we need to generate an internal sense of safety for ourselves. Doing this means that the processes of thinking and learning can begin. Thinking can be done as an individual, a pair, or a group — if properly organised, perhaps even as an entire organisation or social system. Learning about yourself as an individual or group involves a growing pain that must be tolerated if we are to develop as leaders and teams.

Wilfred Bion[30] described a "hatred of learning by experience" that must be overcome if we are to see what is really going on. Very often in group coaching or on leadership development programmes, groups resist thinking and want to be told, to be taught. They seek a knowing leader in the form of the group facilitator and want them to tell them what to do and how to do it. In doing so, they negate their own capacity as a group to think. What's needed is reflection and personal inquiry, as you explore what your part in your situation is, as an individual and a group. Learning in this way means surrendering to this experience even when it is intensely unpleasant, sacrificing an idea you have of how things are in the name of the truth about yourself and your organisational system.

Crucially, this process of thinking from a third position changes your and/or the group's relationship to anxiety. You are no longer "anxious", you are now the observer of anxiety, either in yourself or the others, or both. You have become what Larry Hirschhorn calls the 'observing ego'[31]. This reorientation is central to becoming an anxiety-aware leader. It doesn't mean you no longer feel the anxiety. It means that you have a different relationship with it — one where your identity and your feelings are no longer conflated, allowing you to step back from your immediate emotional experience and review the meaning of your anxiety.

Thinking: real thinking is founded on a connection with reality and a rejection of the imagined fantasy we create to soften or deny it. It means finding a space in your mind from where you can view things objectively. Considering your internal processes, including your feelings, through an objective lens can help you ask questions such as: what is the source of my emotional response? and is it still relevant today? How should I be in this situation and what questions should I ask? From this vantage point, it is also possible to learn about your outer system — to reflect on what is going on and what these events might mean. This work involves interrupting the events that occur inside you and in your operating environment, to work out your part in them and learn.

Your thinking should go beneath the surface; this means thinking about how the unconscious is at play. What is it that is driving your behaviour, or that of the group, that may not be easy to see — something at work in the system but hidden from view? This is often a defence against anxiety. Asking how the group is defending itself against anxiety is always a great question, as is "what is this in service of?" This second question helps you interrupt what is driving behaviour (in you or the group) and see something useful that is out of your awareness. Thinking together with others can accelerate your learning. The role of the leader is to create the conditions or rather the containment necessary for thinking together to take place. This means creating safe bounded spaces where members of an organisation can reflect, think, and learn together. It may be that a discernible action is arrived at through this process, or it may be that the anxiety is worked through, and more trust and safety is created as a result.

3. Act

The output of pausing and thinking is acting. However, it is conscious action, action that is grounded in the reality of what is happening inside you and your external environment. For instance, if you can see (from a third position) that your reaction to an event is a result of an unconscious message picked up in childhood, you have the possibility of choosing not to do it. Without this awareness, you will mechanically react to events in the same way you have always done. This action is likely not in service of your task, it's in service of relieving yourself of the pain of your experience.

Seeing what is going on in the system, unencumbered by anxiety, allows you to be conscious or choiceful in action.

Whilst doing can be an important aspect of leadership, getting stuff done may not always be in service of your task, the task of leadership. The process of thinking might result in the learning that was needed for you to be different, as opposed to doing something differently. Ways to be when leading with anxiety are covered in Chapter 4.

> **Warning**: thinking and acting need to be thoroughly tested. Freud's pleasure principle is consistently present, working to take you away from reality and help you find a more comfortable place. This testing need not create further anxiety but should rather act as a check on your thinking.

By employing these skills in an integrated sequence or cycle, it is possible to change your relationship with anxiety and use it as a prompt for reflection and inquiry. Without it you become the anxiety, and it takes the reins. This model describes a process of creating containment for yourself as a leader or for followers — a task that requires you to work on yourself and build self-awareness. This self-leadership will be covered in more depth in Chapter 6. Before that, we must consider how this leadership skill can be supported by structures within organisations: the boundaries of authority, role, and task.

Figure Two: Pause, Think, Act as an Open System

The diagram below illustrates the pause, think, act method as an open system. Imagine noticing the feeling of anxiety in your body. It shows up as a worry or agitation; it indicates friction between your inner world and the external environment. Start by noticing the heat of this friction and then take in the anxiety.

Containing it, you make it available for examination — on your own or as a group. It is then possible to think what this anxiety might mean and work out what to do with or about it.

Figure Two

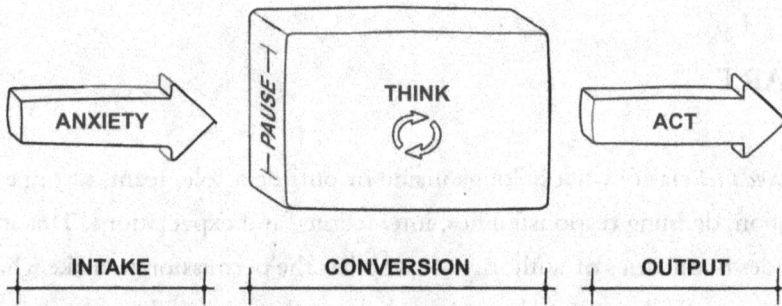

Building a Structure That Contains

Leaders have a clear role, perhaps even a primary role, to contain their followers' anxiety. In doing so, they create a sense of safety that cultivates creativity and cooperation. The aware-leader method offers a practical framework for how to lead with anxiety. However, organisations can also provide their members with structural containment through having a clear purpose, roles and responsibilities that are understood, and an operating model and business processes that offer an unambiguous way of working. These structural elements of an organisation provide boundaries between, for example, where a manager's authority starts and ends, or the scope of a team or project. Structure works with culture; it is suffused with organisational conventions and behaviour and can be a source of containment or uncertainty, depending on how well these boundaries are drawn.

A helpful way of thinking about structure in organisations is the BART framework — **b**oundary, **a**uthority, **r**ole, and **t**ask. Thinking 'BART' provides a valuable structure for leaders seeking to create a containing environment that helps hold anxiety and maintain focus on the task within organisations.

This framework is explained below:

BART

Boundaries clarify what belongs inside or outside a role, team, or organisation, defining responsibilities, interactions, and expectations. This includes boundaries of authority — who has the permission to make what decisions. Well-managed boundaries balance flexibility with clarity, reducing confusion and anxiety. Leaders play a key role in maintaining these boundaries, monitoring overlaps or blurred responsibilities that can lead to inefficiency and stress. Leadership, in this sense, is an activity that takes place on the boundary.

Authority refers to the legitimacy to make decisions and act within a role, derived both from formal structures, such as titles, and informal sources, such as trust. Leaders must be mindful that authority is co-created — it relies not only on formal authorisation but also on how they are perceived and supported by others. Effective leaders navigate tests to their authority through transparency and boundary management.

Roles are shaped by both formal responsibilities and informal dynamics, encompassing expectations and relational functions. Role clarity stabilises teams, while ambiguity can lead to burnout and frustration. Leaders must clarify their own roles and support team members in defining theirs, being aware of unconscious pressures that may lead individuals to take on informal roles driven by group dynamics.

Tasks define the core purpose of an organisation, yet these can shift due to external pressures, such as crises or regulatory demands. Alongside the formal task, hidden tasks may emerge from unspoken anxieties or reputational concerns. Leaders must maintain alignment with their primary task, while addressing these hidden dynamics to sustain focus and adaptability.

By attending to BART, leaders create a scaffolding that contains organisational anxiety, fostering a resilient, clear, and purpose-driven environment.

The Uncontained Organisation

It's possible to imagine working in an organisation that does not have the structure described above in place. What might it feel like not knowing your task, not knowing who's in charge, and not having a clear role? By being increasingly anxiety-aware, leaders can see how they and their followers defend against difficult feelings. Without this awareness, we are at risk of looking at the world through an anxious lens that obscures the picture and inhibits organisations from fulfilling their task.

A Leadership Story

Unheld is a story that captures the emotional undercurrent of leadership in fast-paced, high-pressure environments. It's not just about job roles and reporting lines — it's about what happens when leaders and their teams feel untethered, left to navigate unclear expectations with little support. Lizzie's experience highlights a common challenge: how can leaders lead well when they themselves feel adrift? This story serves as an invitation to consider the ripple effects of unclear structures, unacknowledged anxiety, and a lack of containment. As you read, reflect on the subtle moments when things could have been different — when a conversation, a pause, or a gesture of genuine interest might have shifted the narrative. These moments hold powerful lessons about the importance of being held as a leader, so you, in turn, can hold others with confidence and care.

Unheld

Lizzie was excited to begin her new role at an upcoming marketing agency in New York City called Matrix Digital. This was her first executive role where she had responsibility for managing others. The first week was great — meeting new people, drinks after work — the agency felt like a fun place to be. Lizzie's role was a mix of sales and content development, and for this reason, she reported to two people, both vice presidents in the organisation. Lizzie was concerned by this split in reporting but understood it was a small and relatively new agency that needed to optimise its capacity. The pressure to develop new content and generate new business was relentless and came from two directions — two bosses who didn't seem to talk to each other to ensure Lizzie's workload was manageable. The CEO was also very interested in Lizzie's work and would often pull her aside to take on new projects. Unsurprisingly, Lizzie began to work very long hours and take her work home with her.

The team Lizzie was responsible for also had multiple reporting lines, as staff worked across functions to give the business the most bandwidth. Lizzie would often go to members of her team with work requests to find that they were already fully allocated with tasks delegated from other managers.

This left her feeling like she didn't have the resources she needed to do the job, and she resented the sense that she was unable to say no to demands from above. Lizzie became increasingly frustrated with her team, as they seemed occupied with other managers' work; these frustrations seeped out in emails and conversations, and she became more and more distant from the people she managed.

Feeling stressed and anxious, she went to the person she believed was her line manager. Sarah was the chief design officer and the person who approved Lizzie's leave. During their meeting, Sarah only occasionally looked up from her computer screen, and at one point, she stopped and looked at Lizzie to tell her she might need to put her "big girl pants on" if she's going to be a success at Matrix. After nearly three months in her new role, Lizzie felt lost and confused, uncertain about her role and reporting lines across the organisation. The meeting with Sarah had made her feel unsafe and vulnerable, and she decided to talk to a colleague called Ben about her predicament. Ben's experience was similar to Lizzie's, and he bemoaned an uncaring leadership that failed to support or provide adequate direction, saying, "They just don't want to listen to how things are, and we have no strategy." Whilst this added to Lizzie's frustration, she also found comfort in finding a fellow traveller who gave permission to locate the responsibility for what was going on with a leadership team obsessed with rapid business growth.

***

When we think about what might be going on with Matrix Digital, it's easy to imagine the top leaders working hard to generate new business. This work brings leaders into contact with the organisation's external environment, the marketplace of potential new clients. Leaders meet these clients at the boundary of their organisational system and experience the possibility of failure, of not making sales. The anxiety generated at the boundary, in the example of Matrix, appears then to be pushed down into the organisation in the form of pressure and unrealistic expectations on staff. This fast-moving agency had asked Lizzie to help win new business and create content for marketing campaigns; given the scale of each task as the business grew, this was experienced as an impossible workload.

Overwhelmed, Lizzie began to feel anxious but was unable to find support from her boss. Sarah was deeply ambitious and focused on success; this way of being left little time for the task of leadership, and when Lizzie had shared her feelings, Sarah was unavailable for her. Listening would have meant facing the reality of the organisation and the impossible task that Lizzie had been given. By denying the reality of the context in this way, Sarah was able to defend against the anxiety of what was going on. In her "big girl pants" comment, we see Sarah project her own sense of being out of her depth, and not mature enough for the job, into Lizzie. Unable to think about how she herself might be struggling in her role, she blocks Lizzie out and evacuates her own difficult feelings of not being good enough. This comment also portrays a collusion with a patriarchal industry that expects women to take on conventional masculine traits of toughness if they are going to fit in and be accepted. We can imagine how Sarah's emotional unavailability and implied criticism made Lizzie feel, contributing to a sense of not being held.

The link to how Lizzie then relates to her own team is perhaps easy to see. Her anxiety is expressed through how she communicates as she reacts to her experience of life at Matrix. It's not until she shares her frustrations with her colleague that she finds some comfort. In this dynamic, we can see another splitting in the organisation as middle leaders locate the problem with senior leadership and, in doing so, feel better: the sort of better we feel when we moan to a listening friend about someone or something. Temporarily relieved of anxiety, Lizzie and her colleague add to the dysfunction in the system by putting the problem "out there", setting up a "them and us" dynamic. This sort of defence strategy detracts from the energy available for the task but provides sufficient containment of anxiety for some work to get done, and a status quo can be maintained — at least for a while. Senior leadership in this example is identified as the destination for projections like "it's their fault — they don't understand". This defence is enabled by a sense of "other" — outside a personal, group, or organisation boundary. In this case, the split was between middle management and senior leadership; the 'othering' of senior leaders provided Lizzie and her middle management colleagues with good enough containment to carry on.

In the Matrix example, we can see how containment is not simply about clear structure but also about how structure and healthy relationships work in unison. From an emotional point of view, clearly defined structures often operate to contain anxiety and to sustain the psychological space necessary for cooperation and creativity. When structures are unclear, a lack of clarity about tasks, roles, authority, and boundaries gives rise to uncertainty, fear, and anxiety. A boundary around a group or team can offer considerable containment, as people identify with the group and feel a sense of belonging, common focus, and togetherness. This sense of belonging is reinforced by a clear primary task. When the task is clear and understood, it can act as a galvanising glue, or guiding handrail, that promotes cooperation and innovation. When unclear, success is left to chance.

There is little doubt that Matrix would have benefited from clear boundaries in relation to people's roles, authority, and organisation. The lack of this clarity created anxiety for Lizzie that could have been avoided. It was, though, how leaders at Matrix related to this lack of structure that made things worse. This might be especially true as organisational boundaries become increasingly permeable and networked in the face of contextual complexity. Organisations are increasingly having to work across what was previously viewed as a silo to meet the ever-changing demands of new markets. Psychodynamic management consultants Cooper and Dartington[32] suggest that might mean new partnerships that look more like a network than a conventional structure. The importance of how leaders relate to followers at the boundary and the experience of old structures vanishing, as the network emerges, point to a dual task of leadership. Namely, managing one's own anxiety and creating containment for the anxiety of others.

Throughout the Matrix example, we can observe a movement of anxiety similar to Moylan's[33] idea of anxiety contagion and Hirschhorn's[34] description of "the anxiety chain". Anxiety moved around the company into a series of defences that robbed the company of energy, that could have been otherwise used to achieve its goals. The source of this movement seems to have started at the boundary of the organisation and the external environment, where leaders engage with an uncertain marketplace; where the risk of losing a deal or being outpaced by a competitor weighs on the minds of those driving business development — the organisation's hunters. Sales is fraught with psychological danger, rejection, and self-criticism, as well as the possibility of ego inflation and a feeling of omnipotence as you close the big deal and "kill the prey". In this case, leaders could not contain the anxiety of business development, and it flooded an organisation that had failed to assemble the emotional scaffolding necessary to provide effective containment: a clear purpose, role descriptions that people understood, and reporting lines that worked. In the absence of the apparatus of containment, a chain reaction of anxiety was started that led to a process of denial, splitting, and projection that, left unexamined, kept the system just where it was — stuck.

***

The Contained Organisation

Most of us know what it feels like when your boss and your team has your back, and what a safe organisation feels like. It might feel like a secure family, with caring parents and siblings who are fun to play with and tolerably rivalrous. Perhaps a safe family would include friendly aunts and uncles, and helpful family friends. Rules and conventions would be clear and managed lovingly, like what time you have to be home, where you could and couldn't go, or the acceptable language spoken at home. We can all intuit how a family that knows its purpose, has clear boundaries, supports and loves its members might feel; organisations are the same. Organisations, like families, that are without good enough structure, can feel unsafe, and normal anxiety is not contained. This leads to dysfunctional dynamics that get in the way of you performing your task.

The idea of being 'held' or 'contained' has found its way into the lexicon of popular psychology from its roots in psychoanalysis. Bion's[35] concept of container-contained described how a leader holds and processes a group's anxieties, transforming them into something more manageable. This psychoanalytical idea explains how leadership contains difficult emotions, reducing anxiety and enabling thought. As we become more literate in the language of self-help and psychology, these terms have increasingly shown up in our conversations, especially at work. Perhaps this is seen most clearly in contemporary organisations in the concept of 'psychological safety'; the term was coined by Harvard Professor Amy C. Edmondson in 1999. Her definition:

People who feel psychologically safe are confident that candour and vulnerability are welcome in their workplace. They believe that they will not be punished or humiliated for speaking up with ideas, questions, concerns, or mistakes, and that the team is safe for inter-personal risk-taking.

It's obvious to see how not speaking up, asking questions, raising concerns, or making mistakes could easily be counter to an organisation's mission, and the creativity and cooperation necessary to achieve it. Uncertain about how the system might respond, we stay quiet, don't cooperate, and are unable to think creatively. Arguably a pioneer of psychological safety, British psychoanalyst Donald Winnicott[36] first used the term 'holding environment' to describe the optimal environment for what he called "good enough parenting". By facilitating this holding environment, the mother was able to insulate her baby from stress, carefully selecting the moments to allow the ordinary frustrations of life into the child's experience. The mother gradually increased the time between the child expressing a need and meeting that need, building the infant's capacity to manage her emotions. Bion's similar but theoretically distinct concept of the 'container' explains how the mother receives unwanted or overwhelming projections from the child, processes them, and returns the experience in a modified or digestible way, building on Klein's concept of projective identification. Much of what we understand of psychological safety is founded on these ideas of holding and containment, and they are vital to the task of leadership.

A Leadership Story

Held is a story about what happens when someone offers genuine presence in a moment of distress. Unlike organisational fixes or formal meetings, this is about the quiet power of listening — an act that can feel small but often holds immense weight. In this story, Lizzie's struggle continues to escalate, yet a simple encounter with a colleague changes the emotional tone of her experience. It doesn't provide instant solutions, but it does offer something just as valuable: the chance to feel seen, understood, and steady enough to take the next step forward. As you read, notice how Sam's calm and contained approach helps Lizzie move from emotional overwhelm to constructive reflection. This story illustrates that sometimes the most impactful thing we can do as leaders— or colleagues — is not to fix but to simply hold space, allowing others to process their feelings and find clarity in their own time.

Held

Things at Matrix Digital weren't getting any better for Lizzie, but she did find some solace in her relationship with Ben. Both found themselves complaining about management at the agency and were caught up in a "them and us" story that they told each other to explain their experience at work. This story was helpful and a source of humour and connection for Lizzie, but it also felt unsatisfactory. She felt alone with her situation and couldn't see a way out.

The dual pressure to sell and oversee content generation mounted until it got too much, and Lizzie found herself experiencing an overwhelming sense of panic. On one occasion, she retreated to the bathroom in tears when she almost collided with Sam, the head of Finance. Sam, concerned about Lizzie's obvious distressed state, invited her to a breakout area where they could talk. He gave her a glass of water and asked her, "What's happening?"

Lizzie went on to describe her experience of starting work at Matrix and how she had found the lack of clarity about her role and those of the people she managed very difficult. This, and the pressure to both sell and produce content with insufficient resources in the team, had become unbearable. Sam experienced Lizzie as distraught, as she offloaded all her worries onto him. Sam could feel the pain that Lizzie was experiencing as she explained how she was feeling tearful and angry, pouring out her heart. Sam listened quietly to Lizzie, remaining calm and still. He offered no advice and only a few words of acknowledgement. After speaking for nearly 20 minutes, Lizzie noticed she was calming down and was more able to tolerate her feelings. It was as if Sam had shared her emotional burden, and things felt better; she put this down to the old adage "a problem shared is a problem halved".

As Lizzie slowed down, Sam asked, "If you were giving yourself advice, what would you say?"

"Good question," Lizzie replied. "Quit and get a new job," was her first response, which they both laughed at. Then she said, "I guess I should start by explaining to my bosses what's going on for me and how I'm feeling." Sam resisted the temptation to jump in with his views regarding what she should do and sat quietly with Lizzie as she thought about what might be needed. Lizzie used this space to go on to analyse her predicament, noting how poor role definition, a lack of business direction, not knowing how her team was organised, or who she really reported to were all creating considerable pressure that was becoming overwhelming. Sam then asked, "What do you think the first step is?" and Lizzie replied, "I'm going to write down my thoughts and then," (she said with a smile) "book a meeting with both my bosses to tell them what's going on for me ..."

***

In the story above, we see how Sam can offer himself as a container for Lizzie. Lizzie heaped her troubles onto (or into) Sam, and he held himself together to simply be alongside her. By remaining calm and present to Lizzie's emotions, Sam was able to offer a reverie for Lizzie. It took two minds for the raw emotions to be processed or digested, facilitating an opportunity for the experience to be thought about. Sam's help seemed to make all the difference. Something somatic or bodily took place. Sam felt Lizzie's suffering in his body as she expressed her feelings. It was as if Lizzie poured her heart out into Sam's heart. By providing a container for her feelings and maintaining a calm state of being, Sam helped Lizzie process her difficult feelings in the same way that a mother provides reverie for her distressed child. This is not to imply that Lizzie was infantile in her behaviour; rather, we humans have always needed help to process difficult emotions. It may have been that something in this situation at work unconsciously activated a memory from childhood, that made this particular set of circumstances more difficult for Lizzie. We all have a personal history, damaged bits of ourselves that can be mobilised by our circumstances in ways we can't easily identify. In these moments, we are transported to a more infantile or childlike state of development and are unable to bring to bear the adult capacities we rely on to be effective at work. Often, we can see this in our relationships with people in authority in our organisation, when we attribute the characteristics of our parents to our bosses in a way that twists the relationship in an often-unhelpful fashion.

By asking the question, "If you were giving yourself advice, what would you say?" Sam invited Lizzie to form a different perspective, a place in her mind that she could step into sideways from which to look at things. This invitation was to think reflexively. To be reflexive involves thinking from within experiences or, as the Oxford English Dictionary puts it, "turned or reflected back upon the mind itself". The question evoked rational thinking that put a little distance between what she had invested personally and her logic. This whole process could be put down to: Sam calmed her down and she was able to think clearly. In a sense, this is true, and it also perhaps discounts what Sam did as a leader, both for Lizzie individually and for the organisational culture. In organisations under considerable pressure, it may be that the containment Sam offered Lizzie is vital to effective functioning. This is not to confuse the role of leader with the 'mental health first aider', but highlights the leader's task of containing the anxiety within the system.

***

Making Sense

Out of the grip of anxiety, the task of making sense of our thoughts, sensations, and feelings comes to the fore. Noticing the micro-dynamics in the team, as well as the political movements in the macro-system, leaves us with a riddle. David Armstrong's[37] concept of the organisation-in-the-mind is a key idea in systems-psychodynamic thinking that can help us with this puzzle. Our organisation-in-the-mind can be seen as an internalised image of our organisation. Individuals do not just relate to the actual organisation they work in, but to an internalised version of it — shaped by their personal experiences, projections, anxieties, and unconscious assumptions. It's as if we all walk around our organisations with a different idea about what our organisation is and how it works: an image seen through the lens of our own unconscious. This internal model influences how we think, feel, and behave in organisational life, in ways often beyond our conscious awareness. The organisation-in-the-mind is not a rational or objective representation but is shaped by emotions, past experiences, and relationships with authority and structures. It is influenced by anxiety, hope, past organisational roles, and even childhood experiences of authority and dependency.

Leaders need to recognise that when individuals describe "the organisation", they are often describing their own internal experience of it, which may or may not align with reality. Understanding these unconscious images can help in diagnosing organisational culture, leadership dynamics, and sources of resistance or dysfunction. The organisation-in-the-mind is not static; it is constantly being reshaped through interactions, organisational changes, and group dynamics. A leader might describe their organisation as "rigid and bureaucratic", yet when explored further, this perception may stem from their own anxieties about authority or past experiences in hierarchical institutions. Another leader might view the same organisation as "chaotic and fragmented", reflecting a different internalised experience.

Armstrong's[38] model invites us to make sense of what is going on in the self and system, to see what is really shaping our view of the organisation, consciously and unconsciously. An exercise that can help make sense of your organisation-in-the-mind is drawing. This involves illustrating your concept of your organisation held in mind on paper. The exercise can work well in groups when you follow the steps below.

Organisation-in-the-Mind

1. Create a calm and receptive state within the group, where its members are relaxed and feel able to express themselves openly.

2. Each member of the group draws their organisa-tion-in-the-mind. It's good to use lots of different materials, pens, pencils, crayons, glitter — get creative! The group should take the time they need. It can help to invite the group to draw their emotional picture of the organisation.

3. When the drawings are complete, lay them out on the floor then go around as a group to study each one. After a short period of reflection, the group should 'free associate' with the picture — saying what comes to mind as they look at it. This should be done in an unfiltered way to best elicit unconscious meaning. It's helpful to ask the illustrator to locate themselves in the drawing using a symbol that represents them.

4. Once the group members have all expressed what sense

they make of the drawing, using free association and reflection, the person who drew the picture should say what they
were trying to illustrate; they should describe their organisation-in-the-mind.

5.   In turn, go around to each illustration and then return to the
     group, arranged in a circle, to make sense of people's associa-
     tions and reflections, trying to remember to think about how
     anxiety and defences against anxiety might be showing up.

The picture below is an example of an organisation-in-the-mind drawing.
What sense do you make of it?

Figure Three

By reflecting on the illustration above, it is possible to associate to the
image. I think it looks like a cage or prison with different aspects of the
organisation in each cell. A heart, perhaps, represents emotion or love; the

sun indicates light or hope; there are dashes of red demonic eyes hiding in the shadows. The blue lines coming from one box remind me of a waterfall or could they possibly represent Rapunzel's hair dropped down to enable a rescue? The image in the bottom left could be an endless spiral or a snail. And the blob on the right could be an ear, trapped also — perhaps something is not being heard.

The associations that people make are personal and they can often connect with something unconscious, shared or held within the group. When this happens, new insights can be found, or sometimes things are communicated that were impossible to talk about before. When the illustrator reveals what it is that represents them in the drawing, we get to hear about how they see themselves in the organisation, consciously or perhaps unconsciously. Working within this context can help you enter a conversation at a deeper level, and make sense together about what is going on and where anxiety is showing up.

This exercise is best completed with a third party, who can see things unencumbered by the pressures of your organisation. When this third party is psychoanalytically orientated in their thinking, they can sometimes bring in unseen dimensions, even drawing on myth and fairy tales that enrich the meaning-making process.

Perhaps, the hair flowing down from the cell in the drawing represents the illustrator's desire to connect with others in the system, or to be less isolated from the external operating environment. It could also represent a desire to reconnect with their own authority and developmental path, as hair can represent personal growth. Whilst these associations may seem a little far out, they can unlock conversations in a way previously not possible, allowing you to identify the anxiety in the system. For example, it may be worth considering what is blocking the illustrator from connecting with others and moving from isolation? Or what might be stopping them from taking up their own authority or developmental journey?

Think Group!

When we experience anxiety we naturally think "I am anxious". This reaction to anxiety is understandable but it ignores the possibility of projective identification. This refers to the idea that you are experiencing something of the others' emotional experience; a communication that is being located with you because it is too difficult for them to hold onto and take responsibility for. Focusing on yourself in this way means we ignore how we are being affected by the group. Being anxiety-aware means asking, "Is this my feeling or is it something that is being projected into me by the group?" When something about your experience feels out of place or unusual, this is a prompt to make this inquiry. Thinking about how the group or wider system is affecting your emotional experience provides data to help you work out what is going on. It also unburdens you from the fantasy that it's all your fault and allows you to see how the group is making you feel.

A Space to Reconnect

Sense-making requires space; an anxiety-aware leader creates spaces to reconnect with themselves, with others, and with their task. This leadership practice can be strengthened by engaging with reflective spaces within us, by using the aware-leader method, described in this chapter. Additionally, leaders can foster reflection by establishing physical and psychological spaces within the organisation. These may include dedicated time with a professional coach or consultant, where leaders can work through their experiences in a safe, non-judgemental environment.

Reflective practice groups offer another vital avenue for reflection and containment, especially in complex relational work. Originally developed in clinical and caregiving contexts, these groups have been adapted across organisational settings to support teams and individuals in navigating uncertainty, anxiety, and relational dynamics. Such groups serve as regular touchpoints for leaders to consider not just the technical aspects of their roles, but also the emotional and relational undercurrents influencing their leadership.

Reflective Groups

Reflective practice groups are not performance reviews or operational meetings. Instead, they are facilitated spaces where leaders can slow down, step back, and think critically about the dynamics at play in their work.

These sessions are characterised by:

- **Containment and Emotional Processing:** facilitators help leaders make sense of the 'projections' they encounter — difficult emotions and anxieties that may be passed on from the wider system.
- **Relational Understanding:** group members explore their responses to relational tensions, fostering a deeper understanding of team dynamics and reducing unhelpful behaviours such as 'splitting', where different parts of a team become polarised in response to conflict.
- **Shared Learning and Support:** by sharing and reflecting on experiences, participants develop a collective awareness of the challenges they face and strengthen their capacity for thoughtful, contained action.

As highlighted throughout this book, unprocessed anxiety can lead leaders to adopt defensive behaviours — such as micro-management or avoidance — that undermine trust and engagement. Reflective spaces provide an antidote to these dynamics, encouraging leaders to confront their uncertainties without being overwhelmed by them.

By normalising reflection as part of their leadership practice, leaders cultivate resilience and adaptability, even in high-pressure contexts. As one facilitator observed, the goal is not to "solve" every issue in the room but to create an environment where new insights can emerge and be metabolised. Leaders leave such sessions not necessarily with quick answers but with a renewed sense of clarity, purpose, and connection to their values. Reflective spaces, whether one-on-one or in groups, remind us that thoughtful leadership is not a solitary act but a relational practice that draws strength from vulnerability, curiosity, and the capacity to stay present in the face of complexity.

Key Takeaways

1. **Anxiety as Leadership Intelligence.**
   Anxiety isn't just an obstacle — it's a source of insight. Leaders who engage with, rather than suppress, anxiety develop greater self-awareness and emotional resilience. An anxiety-aware leader treats anxiety as a signal, not a threat, allowing for intentional, steady leadership in uncertain times.

2. **Pause, Think, Act – A Framework for Leadership Anxiety**
   - **Pause**: interrupt automatic reactions. Create stillness to notice and contain anxiety before it dictates responses.
   - **Think**: anxiety distorts perception. Step back, reflect, and gain clarity — both individually and within teams.
   - **Act**: move with intention, not reactivity. Sometimes this means taking bold action; other times, it's holding steady or engaging in tough conversations.

3. **Containment as a Core Leadership Function**
   Leaders who hold their own anxiety create space for others to manage theirs. When left unchecked, anxiety spreads, leading to avoidance, splitting, and projection. Leaders can modify team anxiety by holding and processing emotions rather than transmitting them.

4. **Organisational Structures Shape Anxiety**
   Anxiety isn't just personal — it's systemic. The BART framework (**b**oundary, **a**uthority, **r**ole, **t**ask) helps assess whether structures provide containment. Without clear roles and authority, anxiety floods the system, leading to dysfunction and mistrust.

5. **Reflection Builds Resilience**

   Containment isn't avoidance — it's about creating the time and space to process difficult emotions. Organisations that prioritise reflective spaces through coaching, team dialogue, and leadership development foster clarity, confidence, and systemic thinking. Anxiety, when engaged with thoughtfully, becomes a tool for insight and growth.

Chapter Four

Ways of Being

"Being human means being thrown into a world we did not choose, yet still being called to take responsibility for our own existence."

Martin Heidegger[39]

Often the thing that occupies a leader's attention is what to do. There is invariably pressure to do something, from the board, your boss, your peers, staff, and other stakeholders. Perhaps the greatest pressure to act comes from within, when we self-generate a pressure to do something; to make some progress — any progress. Resisting this invitation is perhaps counter to the prevailing advice about leadership, which is all about getting stuff done. It's not that doing isn't important or indeed necessary, but it might not always be leadership at all. The role of the leader may not be about doing but rather creating an environment where stuff gets done. If this is what leadership is about, then thinking about and developing our 'being' might be helpful. In this chapter, we consider some ways to be when leading with anxiety.

Be Compassionate

The idea of compassionate leadership has become increasingly popular in contemporary thinking about organisations; an approach that has been championed by many institutions, including the National Health Service in England. Compassion can be defined as "a sensitivity to suffering in self and others, with a commitment to try to alleviate and prevent it"[40]. We can experience compassion in different ways: we can feel compassion for other people; we can experience compassion from others; and there is also the compassion we can direct towards ourselves. The origins of the word indicate a further layer of understanding. From Latin, compassionem means "sympathy" or "to feel pity", from com "with, together". By the 14th century, the word's literal meaning was: "suffering with another". This original meaning of the word points to something that takes two people — a sufferer and a companion on the path.

What happens to the suffering when someone suffers alongside us? If we ask this question of ourselves, we can probably sense how something is soothed, that our suffering becomes more bearable and somehow easier to process. It is as if the substance of the suffering is in some way changed; it feels materially different when our emotional burden is shared, compared to suffering alone. We can also see that it isn't when someone with the best intentions tries to fix our problems for us, giving a hundred solutions or telling us, "It's going to be OK." This may have the opposite effect, frustrating us and increasing the feeling of isolation. Compassion goes beyond simply being listened to; something more is happening — but what?

By thinking psychoanalytically, we can imagine how a mother suffers alongside her child, in a way that might start to explain what happens to us when we experience compassion. Projective identification was referred to previously as a means of psychological transformation; seen through the lens of the mother's compassion, she modifies the child's feelings, making them more manageable. In this way, the mother's state of reverie offers the child containment and allows her to modify the infant's difficult experience on the infant's behalf.

The idea of reverie as a practice is well established in psychoanalysis; it has been defined as "the therapist's receptive, containing state of mind, which they can use to help clients transform unprocessed mental contents into useful elements from which they can learn"[41]. This maternal or parental practice has been employed by psychotherapists and psychoanalytically orientated management consultants; we can also imagine the possibility of a leader providing containment for a follower in this way, something that comes naturally to some as they aspire to be more compassionate. This sort of leadership was illustrated in the leadership story Held, told above. In this way, leaders like Sam vicariously process the raw feelings of the distressed person, as they sit alongside them and experience their suffering with them.

Klein[42] noted that infants communicate their raw emotions by, for example, crying. In response, the mother or caregiver takes the infant's state of mind into their own mental space. Rather than deny these feelings of distress and get rid of her feelings through projection, the mother contains the infant's experience. She tries to imagine what might be happening to the infant to give it some meaning. In this way, the mother tolerates the child's distress and can help the child process their feelings. Imagine a baby waking from a nap crying and distressed. The mother holds the child, comforts them, and assumes they are hungry. The mother proceeds to feed the baby. The child experiences the mother as calm and receptive. If the child could speak, they might say: "When I woke up, I thought that something terrible was happening to me, but you didn't seem to think it was a big deal; I was just hungry. So that's what hunger feels like!" The baby requires a caregiver who can tolerate her anxiety, and the caregiver trains the baby to process or digest their difficult feelings.

This process probably takes place hundreds of times each day, slowly helping the infant to build up a mental apparatus to think. For Bion, this relationship between the mother and the infant represents a dyad — or partnership — where the pair grow together through their ability to tolerate doubt until some meaning is attributed to it. In this way, the relationship facilitates learning and growth through the model mentioned previously, which he called container-contained. This model of development was later used in the relationship between a psychoanalyst and their patient. In this space, the analyst acts as a container and must be capable of reverie to accept and metabolise raw emotions before giving them back to the patient in a digestible form. As we have seen with Sam's leadership in the Held leadership story, this technique can also be used by leaders.

Central to this idea is the principle that another mind is needed to help process thoughts and emotions, and make them available for thinking. The other mind is originally that of the mother or caregiver, and this process was then adopted to be used in psychoanalysis. Psychoanalytically orientated consultants and coaches also endeavour to employ containment and reverie in their practice. A superpower, perhaps, and something Bion observed as a central task of parenthood in his description of maternal reverie: an act of compassion or love that helps someone process their feelings and allows them to think about their experience.

Be Vulnerable

Originally from the Latin vulnus, or "wound", the word vulnerable literally means the act of showing your wound. Knights of old who could walk outside without their armour were said to be vulnerable. To do this took the confidence to leave the chainmail and plate armour back at the castle. The same courage may be required today to walk about your organisational system without the defences provided by position, power, and privilege. It might now be necessary to show your wound, your vulnerability, and in doing so expose your humanity. In his 1997 book Reworking Authority, Larry Hirschhorn[43] offers a model for how we need to change our relationship with authority in organisations, if we are to successfully negotiate uncertainty. Hirschhorn argues that contemporary organisations require that individuals at all levels make themselves more open to one another. He warns of the stark reality that people don't do this because they risk looking incompetent and feeling ashamed.

Threat and risk always mobilise our fantasies about authority; our forgotten feelings of dependence on parents and teachers come to the surface. Will they protect us, hurt us, or divide us? The fear that leaders may abandon their own responsibilities and blame staff can show up to interfere with people's adult capacities. Equally, staff can hate their leaders even when they are protecting them from the perceived threat. All these behaviours, of course, have the fingerprints of anxiety smeared across them, and make the task of responding to the threat even harder. Instead, Hirschhorn asserts we must develop a culture of openness in which leaders, followers, and peers make themselves vulnerable to one another as a precondition for confronting the external challenges they face. This venture, of course, exposes people directly to anxiety, the worry of your status and position being eroded, and the fantasy or perhaps reality that you might lose your job.

The task, then, is for leaders to cultivate a new relationship with followers where their hero or parent status is abandoned, and a culture of openness is created. Leaders must risk their apparent authority and take off their armour in the interest of deepening their substantive authority. Followers, for their part, must overcome their excessive dependence on leaders and elevate themselves from what psychiatrist Eric Berne[44] called a 'Child ego state'; a relationship defined by dependency and a position in the mind that inflates leaders and their ability. In moving away from this ego state, followers learn the leadership they are required to follow, and both leaders and followers prime themselves for new possibilities.

The nature of contemporary problems in our uncertain world means that the natural instinct to increase control doesn't work. As we tighten our grip in one area, another part of the system reacts in a way we did not predict. So-called wicked problems, typical of the 21st-century milieu, simply do not respond in the same way as before. The preparation necessary for this sort of 'being' to take place involves a close encounter with anxiety, both for leaders and their followers, where the importance of organisational containment is elevated. To lead in this way requires personal growth, and growing doesn't come without pain. It requires leaders to refrain from using their positional power as a defence against the anxiety of knowing the other. This means that leaders must acknowledge their dependence on others and become open to the help they need from the system. Larry Hirschhorn put it like this: "They must step beyond their formal roles and present themselves to their subordinates as human beings, having not just strengths but also limits and uncertainties." In other words, leaders must lead in a way that acknowledges their vulnerability, thereby inviting followers in as equals and partners in a creative task.

Be Courageous

Our ability to experience anxiety and stay with it, as Sam did in the leadership story earlier, is neither natural nor easy. The impulse to escape, to suppress, or to act rashly in response to discomfort is deeply ingrained in the psyche. Yet, this capacity to remain with our experience — without being consumed by it — is essential to the containing process of reverie and to the kind of leadership that can make sense of what is happening in an organisational system. This quality is elusive; we recognise it in the leaders we admire most, in those with whom we have worked, and sometimes in public figures who seem to exude a rare steadiness in times of crisis. It feels like something they have and I do not. Yet, courage is not a fixed trait; it is a practice, a stance, a way of orienting ourselves toward uncertainty.

Rudyard Kipling's famous words "If you can keep your head when all about you are losing theirs" capture something of this steady, grounded presence. When chaos, fear, and anxiety surge through an organisation, those who can contain themselves provide something invaluable: not the eradication of anxiety, but the ability to hold it, to think with it, to remain intact rather than react. Ernest Hemingway famously defined courage as "grace under pressure", a phrase first used in a 1929 interview with Dorothy Parker for The New Yorker magazine. It speaks to an ability to maintain composure under strain, not by denying fear, but by integrating it — by making it something that can be carried, rather than something that must be expelled. Yet, this notion of grace should not be confused with a rigid stoicism that suppresses emotion in favour of appearing strong. True courage is neither about masking vulnerability nor indulging it, but about holding oneself together without retreating into defensiveness or avoidance.

Looking at the etymology of courage offers another layer of meaning. The word courage stems from the Latin cor, meaning heart. The deeper origins trace back to the Indo-European kerd, meaning not just heart but also valour — the quality of mind that enables one to meet danger without being paralysed by fear. Yet, the phrase "without fear" is deceptive. True courage is not the absence of fear but the capacity to act in the presence of it. From a psychoanalytic perspective, fear and anxiety are unavoidable; the challenge is not to eliminate them but to find a way to stay with them without falling into defensive reactions. The leader who feels compelled to act immediately, to remove uncertainty through premature decision making, is often unconsciously attempting to rid themself of anxiety rather than tolerating it. Leadership, in this sense, is a form of emotional containment — not just for the leader, but for the organisation as a whole.

Wilfred Bion argued that the greatest psychological challenge in times of stress is to resist the evacuation of thought. When anxiety rises, the mind seeks relief — often by splitting off the discomfort and projecting it elsewhere. This process, if unchecked, leads to impulsivity, blame, and emotional contagion, all of which distort reality and impair leadership.

Courage, in this sense, is not merely the endurance of discomfort; it is the willingness to think amid difficulty, to avoid being pulled into reactive states, to hold the anxiety long enough for new insight to emerge. Leadership in an anxious system requires resisting the urge to offload difficult emotions onto others through blame, micro-management, or false certainty. The capacity to hold steady and remain reflective is an act of courage, because it means tolerating one's internal distress while preventing it from seeping into the wider system in a destructive way.

Isabel Menzies Lyth[45], in her seminal work on social defences, described courage as "steadiness under fire." This is distinct from simple resilience, which often suggests an armoured, defensive posture. Instead, steadiness implies something more supple: the ability to withstand external pressures without becoming rigid, to experience stress without shutting down thought. The psychoanalyst Donald Winnicott described a similar phenomenon in childhood development — how an infant, through the presence of a good-enough caregiver, learns to experience distress without fragmentation. This early experience lays the foundation for a capacity to hold oneself together in later life, to meet fear and uncertainty without collapse. Just as a child internalises the soothing presence of a caregiver, leaders must develop the internal resources to soothe themselves, especially when the external world is chaotic and unpredictable. A leader who lacks this internal stability will often seek it externally, leaning too heavily on rules, hierarchy, or authoritarian certainty as a way of imposing order. But this kind of false containment is brittle; it does not allow for genuine thinking or adaption.

John F. Kennedy[46], in Profiles in Courage, cites Hemingway's definition in his exploration of political bravery. The courage Kennedy describes is not about battlefield heroism but about the willingness to stand alone, to risk unpopularity, to hold one's ground when the easier path is to conform. This is the challenge for leaders: not simply to be seen as fearless, but to take responsibility for their emotional responses, to resist the lure of defensive action, and to remain engaged even when anxiety tempts withdrawal. Holding one's ground does not mean stubbornness or blind perseverance; rather, it is about maintaining a thinking stance under pressure, resisting the impulse either to collapse or lash out.

Courage, then, is not about the eradication of fear but about the ability to stay with it. It is the practice of bearing what feels unbearable, of thinking when thought is difficult, of leading not through certainty but through presence. It is the ability to stand still in the storm without numbing, running, or attacking. It is, in Bion's words, the patience to wait for meaning to emerge rather than grasping at easy answers. If anxiety is inevitable, then courage is what allows us to meet it — to step forward, not because we are free of fear, but because we refuse to let fear dictate the path.

A Leadership Story

Leadership is not only about guiding others but also about navigating the deeply personal, often painful, realities that shape one's identity and professional journey. Courage in leadership emerges when individuals confront difficult truths — not just about their external circumstances but also about themselves. This story of Thandiwe, a highly respected leader, illustrates the complex interplay between personal history, institutional structures, and identity.

In a professional landscape where institutional racism often operates as an invisible, insidious force, leaders like Thandiwe must grapple with the emotional cost of systemic inequity. Her story sheds light on the inner work required to disentangle the cumulative weight of these micro-incursions, and the resilience necessary to maintain dignity and composure. This narrative explores how acknowledging vulnerability and engaging with uncomfortable emotions can pave the way for a deeper understanding of oneself and one's capacity to lead with integrity, despite the constraints of an unjust system.

101

The Courageous Leader

Thandiwe is a senior vice president at a global construction firm. She has a significant span of responsibility, and she is well respected in the business. As a rising star, she was selected for a leadership development programme that included one-to-one coaching. It was in the safe space of the coaching that an issue that had been troubling Thandiwe emerged. She described a pattern of behaviour where she would reach a point where she lost her composure and expressed herself angrily, perhaps even aggressively. Thandiwe was concerned that her infrequent but persistent angry outbursts were eroding her relationships with peers and intimidating her team members. She also considered that she might be being seen as an "angry Black woman", and the prospect of this made her sad.

A case of institutional racism had recently hit the headlines in the UK, after a KC's report investigating allegations of racism in a high-profile public body was published. The story was all over the media and had a deep impact on Thandiwe, encouraging her to share her own experience with her coach. Thandiwe's experience of life and organisational life was similar, in that they both involved seemingly incessant exposure to racism. Standing in line at the bank, at the department store, and when trying to complain about poor customer service, it was always there. This experience was very subtle; micro-incursions into Thandiwe's self-esteem that robbed her of dignity in ways that were unnoticeable to some. The activity of racism at work involved being ignored, interrupted, and discounted. It was as if racism was an ambient noise in the background of working life, an emotional tinnitus that constantly agitated her. Her experience was of having to work twice as hard as her white colleagues; she had two master's degrees both from top universities, and this sense of having to overperform had been with her since childhood, installed by her family of origin. On occasion, the racism at work was presented in her awareness, not as background noise that white colleagues could easily dismiss, but as a more discernible discrimination. It was then that she would erupt angrily, afterwards feeling a desire to repair the harm and an accompanying sense of guilt and shame. With her coach, Thandiwe explored what might be happening inside: what emerged was an experience of hyper-vigilance. She was always on high alert, ready for the next abrasive brush with a racist culture. This was exhausting for Thandiwe and required her to mobilise considerable inner resources sometimes, just to show up. Invited to explore where this pattern started, Thandiwe told a story of childhood. She was ten and it was her best friend's birthday, only she hadn't been invited to the party. Days later she saw her friend at school and asked why she wasn't invited; the reply stunned her. Her friend said, "My dad didn't want you there because you're Black." At the time Thandiwe didn't react; confused, she went to her mum who told her to hold her feelings inside and not show them that they affected you.

Years later, in their teens and now at high school, the two girls were playing netball. There was a disagreement on the court between them and Thandiwe uncharacteristically hit her friend. Telling this story Thandiwe saw a process of passivity and rage that had been with her since childhood and was still playing out. Knowing what was going on inside, and how it was affected by the world outside, was useful data but she still felt stuck. She could see how the activity of racism had driven her towards passivity and sometimes it was too much to bear.

***

This leadership story has no happy ending. In those moments of emotional hijack perhaps Thandiwe's only option was to make her excuses and walk away, lest she come into direct conflict with monolithic racism that was impossible for one person to move. This is a frustration of our humanity that would provoke rage in any of us. Thandiwe's courage is obvious; the courage to be despite the infliction of continual anxiety. For me as a white man, this courage is impossible to imagine, and it might be a form of grace under pressure that Black people exercise at work every day, on top of the ordinary pressures of organisational life.

Author and psychologist Guilaine Kinouani[47] talks of how our society and its institutions are perhaps inherently racist, built on a colonial past that's not past at all. Our culture incessantly messaging the idea of white superiority and Black inferiority, often in a way as a white man I fail to notice. This is no emotive assertion, but rather a systemic observation. We see it in our media, art, literature, comedy, education, and language. For me growing up in the 1970s and '80s this seemed more obvious than today. We've made some progress, and the message is still heard as a dog whistle to some, but by others simply unheard. In the UK, we live in a society built on our colonial past. For sure our institutions have adapted to a context where slavery is no longer acceptable, but the roots of many of our major institutions are nearly always entangled in an imperial legacy and dominated by a white culture.

In this context, the trope 'angry Black women' is an interesting one, exquisitely constructed to maintain a system that serves a privileged position. Black women may have a lot to be angry about but by pathologising their behaviour, their expression of something justified is conveniently discounted by a self-protecting system as unregulated and angry. The lesson in this leadership story is not for Black leaders, but an indication of the work that white leaders need to do to change our institutions. This work that would involve taking back the projection of inferiority, and owning the part of ourselves that is racist and benefits from a system stacked in our favour.

Many white leaders claim to be 'anti-racist', and this is likely their conscious view of themselves and their intentions. And perhaps what's needed is the courage to see our racism and take ownership of it. Is it not possible that racist ideas have unconsciously seeped into the psyche and become the building blocks of racist institutions, and in some part shaped the Black experience of organisational life? The leadership challenge is to see something that is hard to see for some and obvious to others. Doing so requires white leaders to expose themselves to potentially overwhelming anxiety, to be vulnerable and courageous enough in the face of their predicament. No easy task perhaps, and without the capacity to withstand the anxiety of our inner racist, racism will remain a Black issue, until white leaders take ownership for their role in how racism is created. Racism is an idea constructed by white people and experienced by Black people. The work of accepting our conscious and unconscious racism, and thinking together how organisations construct and maintain a racist experience, is a task that requires incredible courage from a group that is protected from its destructive consequences; for this reason it is work that, for the most part, remains undone.

***

Be Creative

In a letter to his brothers in 1817, English poet John Keats first used the term Negative Capability, describing the rare ability — "which Shakespeare possessed so enormously" — to accept "uncertainties, mysteries, doubts without any irritable reaching after fact and reason"[48]. This idea challenges the instinctive human response to uncertainty: the compulsion to resolve, to explain, to act. It suggests that creativity emerges not from immediate problem solving, but from the capacity to stay with uncertainty long enough for something new to arise. For leaders, this requires a profound psychological shift: to resist premature certainty; to hold anxiety without rushing to eliminate it; and to tolerate ambiguity until fresh insight emerges.

Leadership is traditionally framed through positive capabilities — skills, competencies, and knowledge that signal authority, mastery, and control. The expectation is that leaders know—that they provide answers, direction, and certainty. "I don't know" is rarely a welcome phrase in organisational life, yet it may be the most honest description of leadership in an unpredictable world. Beneath this expectation lies a deep psychological imprint: our first model of leadership is found in our parents, and our first experience of organisation is the family. As children, we rely on the omniscience of caregivers, believing in their ability to provide safety and order. This early dependency is transferred onto institutions and their leaders — managers, CEOs, political figures — who are unconsciously positioned as parental figures, expected to know to relieve collective anxiety. The fantasy of the hero leader — who dispels uncertainty through decisive action — offers reassurance but can also rob individuals and organisations of their agency.

Yet at the boundary between certainty and uncertainty, something vital happens. A 2001 paper presented at the International Society for the Psychoanalytical Study of Organisations (ISPSO) proposed that leadership requires a balance between positive and negative capabilities. While positive capabilities provide the structure for action, negative capability creates the psychological space necessary for creative thought. Aileen Ward, an American scholar of Keats, suggested that negative capability implies a capacity for containment — the ability to live with ambiguity and paradox, to "remain content with the half knowledge[49]" Containment, in the psychoanalytic sense, does not mean suppressing uncertainty, but holding it — allowing space for thought rather than rushing to action.

This ability to hold space for uncertainty is central to Wilfred Bion's work. Bion suggested that in times of uncertainty, the mind naturally seeks to evacuate anxiety — grasping at premature conclusions to relieve the discomfort of not knowing. Yet Bion argued for a different approach, one that he called patience — a state of mind that echoes the infant's early experience of frustration during weaning. Rather than rushing toward certainty, Bion, like Keats, advocated for a capacity to wait — to sit with the unknown until meaning reveals itself. Kenneth Eisold[50], Ph.D., a psychoanalyst, expands on this, describing negative capability as the ability "to tolerate anxiety and fear, to stay in the place of uncertainty in order to allow for the emergence of new thoughts or perceptions." It is, in essence, a willingness to remain in the dark until new light appears.

This elusive quality — so essential to poets and artists — may be equally essential for leaders navigating an uncertain world. This is not to say that positive capabilities are redundant; in fact, a capability like confidence may be precisely what enables someone to approach the edge of uncertainty rather than retreat from it. Leadership, then, is not about choosing between positive and negative capabilities, but about holding them together — cultivating both the skill to act and the wisdom to wait. Creativity, at its core, is born in this tension, in the space between knowing and not knowing. It requires leaders to orient themselves not toward certainty, but toward the unknown, where insight can emerge, unexpected and transformative.

Be Adaptive

The age of uncertainty seems here to stay, or at least it's uncertain when things will once again return to normal — assuming they ever were. Fortunately, the 2009 book The Practice of Adaptive Leadership introduced a model of leadership seemingly perfect for our uncertain world. The model was developed by Ronald Heifetz, Marty Linsky, and Alexander Grashow[51] at Harvard University's Kennedy School of Government, not to be confused with the Harvard University that sits on the other side of the Potomac River in Washington DC. This groundbreaking model of leadership has many of its roots in the Tavistock tradition, specifically the work of A.K. Rice[52] and his ideas about our relationship to authority and its impact on group dynamics. This approach that starts from the position that our context is uncertain, feels like a step in the right direction for leaders trying to come to terms with the modern world.

Heifetz and co.[53] define adaptive leadership as the practice of mobilising people to tackle tough challenges and thrive. In this definition, we can observe the DNA of the approach. Firstly, let's consider what is meant by a "tough challenge". In adaptive leadership, a distinction is made between adaptive and technical problems and the dynamics that these problems generate. Technical problems are seen as those that can be fixed; the problem is known, and the solution is proven and available. This is not to say the problem is simple, but rather there is a technical solution to it. Adaptive challenges are those where there is no easy answer or readily available solution; the problem is novel, and defining the problem requires some learning. Mobilising people to tackle tough challenges involves what is called 'adaptive work' or the mobilisation of the system to learn. The ability to thrive is about embedding this learning culture in your organisation or community, in a way that supports your ongoing adaption to an ever-changing external environment. It's all about leading effectively in dynamic and challenging environments, where the ability to adapt, learn, and lead through uncertainty is crucial.

Adaptive leadership draws on Ron Britton's[54] idea of the third position in its concept of the balcony. This idea offers a simple but powerful metaphor for developing perspective. Imagine you're on a dance floor at a busy party – the music is loud, the room is packed, and you're caught up in the moment. On the dance floor, it's hard to see the bigger picture: who's dancing with whom; where the room is flowing; and where things might be getting chaotic. You're focused on what's right in front of you. Now, picture stepping up to a balcony overlooking the dance floor. From up there, you can see the whole scene — the patterns of movement; where things are flowing well, and where they're stuck. The balcony offers a view that's impossible to get when you're immersed in the action below.

In leadership, the 'balcony' represents the ability to step back from day-to-day demands and observe what's really happening – within your team, the wider organisation, or even yourself. It's about gaining a clearer sense of the dynamics at play so that you can make more thoughtful, strategic choices rather than reacting emotionally or getting swept up in the noise. Adaptive leadership involves regularly moving between the 'dance floor', where you're actively engaged, and the balcony, where you pause to reflect, adjust, and decide on your next steps. This practice helps leaders respond to complexity with calm, clarity, and purpose rather than being overwhelmed by it. From the balcony, you are able to ask questions that enable you to interpret what might be going on. The following questions are designed to help you think about and, make sense of leadership challenges[55]:

- How do the various partners' distinctive cultures affect how we respectively operate?
- What impact do these cultures have on our ability to deal with our challenge?
- What are our cultural norms, individually and as a partnership, and how do they affect our capacity to deal with our challenge?

These sorts of questions are designed to assist learning, to open the conversation in a way that allows leaders to collectively inquire into the system and examine the challenge together. The very process of doing so promotes knowledge and relieves the anxiety evoked by uncertainty. Learning in this way feels like progress; the body recognises this sort of knowledge, and it erodes uncertainty and soothes the mind. One way of inquiring into the problem is framing it. By framing and reframing, we get to see the problem from different angles, each time distilling it down, hopefully getting closer to its essence.

- Framing might include asking key questions such as:
- Who is facing this problem?
- What is the problem they are facing right now?
- Where does this problem happen?
- When does this problem arise?
- Why is this problem worth solving?

Framing sets out the problem in a way that it can be understood and investigated in service of progress. It is, however, possible to use the task of learning as a way of defending against anxiety. This typically involves a pattern of illustrating or describing the problem without framing it. Illustration is a necessary part of the process of learning but can be the enemy of framing, keeping you stuck in an avoidant loop that temporarily soothes your anxiety by promoting the idea you are doing something and therefore making progress. Ultimately, it is this desire to do something, to act and get the job done, that blocks our capacity to think together and come up with a good enough solution. Thoughtful framing means communicating not just an interpretation of events, although that is helpful, but also something that strikes a chord emotionally with people: a reframe that captures not only facts but also feelings.

Adaptive leadership like the Tavistock approach is about facing the reality of a situation, regardless of the anxiety that it may provoke. Leaders who are in touch with reality often have to communicate what is going on to followers but hopefully do so in a way that keeps people on board. The quote "Leadership is about disappointing people at a rate they can stand" is attributed to Ron Heifetz. His words cut to the heart of leading through uncertainty and change. This quote also highlights a further aspect of adaptive leadership that is helpful when leading with anxiety. It's about recognising that growth often feels like loss, and that people can only tolerate so much disruption before they shut down or push back. This echoes Klein's idea of depressive anxiety — the uncomfortable but necessary state where we acknowledge the impact of our actions on others without collapsing under the guilt. In this state, we face the grief of letting go of old ways of working and the reality that we can't fix everything or please everyone. The leader becomes the vessel or a container, holding the rising pressure of collective anxiety without cracking. The task is to provide enough stability to process discomfort, rather than spilling into blame or paralysis. It's not about removing the turbulence but creating space for it to be experienced without overwhelming those involved.

Ultimately, Heifetz, Linsky and Grashow[56] remind us that "The first step in tackling any adaptive challenge is to get on the balcony so you can see how your organisational system is responding to it". The ability to do this and see the whole is only possible when we change our relationship with our anxiety and see it as data that informs action, rather than a force that sabotages thinking. Being able to observe without controlling every element allows for a richer, more adaptive response to complex challenges. The skill of seeing reality as it is — and not as we imagine it to be — requires us to lead interiorly, something only possible once we accept our role in what is happening and pause to reflect.

Be Hopeful

Hope is not an idle wish nor a naïve optimism that everything will turn out well. It is a practice, a way of orienting oneself toward possibility even in the face of despair. True hope is forged in difficult circumstances. It is both a psychological inheritance and an existential choice, something that is given to us in our earliest relationships and something we must also cultivate through effort, determination, and will. The cultivation of hope is most effective in enduring conditions that feel hopeless. This is when we need to find some resolve to continue, to put one foot in front of the other and make progress no matter how small; each step can represent a move away from despair.

Donald Winnicott saw hope as rooted in the earliest experiences of being held in mind by another. In infancy, when distress arises, an attuned caregiver's presence allows the child to develop the capacity to trust in the future. The infant, unable to soothe themselves, learns through repeated experiences of being comforted that distress does not mean annihilation. Over time, this sense of security becomes internalised, forming the basis for a belief in continuity — the idea that difficulty is not the end, but something that can be endured. Winnicott called this the facilitating environment—a space in which a child can exist, play, and develop without fear of collapse. Within this space, hope emerges not as a guarantee of certainty but as an ability to tolerate the unknown; to believe that something meaningful will come next, if only you can tolerate the anxiety of uncertainty.

For leaders, the task is similar. Just as the infant requires the presence of another to hold their distress, so too do organisations, teams, and individuals look for containment in times of crisis. Hope in leadership does not mean promising an unrealistic outcome, nor does it mean banishing doubt. Instead, it requires creating an environment in which uncertainty can be borne, where the possibility of meaning is kept alive even when the future remains unclear. This kind of leadership is not about providing all the answers, but rather about ensuring that people do not feel abandoned in their searching. For many organisations, providing hope may be a forgotten task of leadership. Something that gets left off the corporate leadership training programme and relegated to an individual duty. If leaders were to think psychodynamically, perhaps they might consider that not all of us had an experience of childhood that included being held in mind: an infancy with sufficient containment to allow us to create a facilitating environment for ourselves. This knowledge might prompt a leader to more proactively perform this function for the system, installing hopefulness when despair prevails. Perhaps, you are a leader who lacked this facility from childhood. Your task may now be to notice the importance of creating this for yourself. This is perhaps the true meaning of growing up, finding our own inner resources to know that difficulties can be endured without fear of collapse.

Viktor Frankl, in Man's Search for Meaning, described hope as an orientation toward meaning, even in suffering. His time in Nazi concentration camps showed him that those who survived were not necessarily the strongest, but those who could locate a sense of purpose in their suffering, however small. He argued that hope is not simply about believing in a better future, but about finding meaning in the present, even when that present is difficult. This task is made more challenging by an imagination that can think the worst and then think of something more horrible, a catastrophising spiral into hell. The mind's capacity to do this is seemingly limitless. I've noticed this myself, without much or even any basis in reality I can imagine a scenario where everything results in disaster. I also notice how things are never as bad as you think. Anxiety does this to us; it can create fantastical possibilities that torment and haunt us. This happens to me more at night and is why I don't believe my thoughts after 8 p.m. - and why I also have a bedtime routine that sets me up for sleep and not sleepless rumination.

Leaders who hold a narrative of purpose amidst uncertainty allow themselves and others to sustain hope — not by denying hardship, but by framing it within a larger story. Hope, in this sense, is not a fragile optimism but a form of endurance, a refusal to collapse into meaningless-ness. What's needed is a bigger story in which to locate your despair, one that doesn't let anxiety get away with negating the fact that this difficulty will end. To do this may require some faith; for Kierkegaard[57], hope is bound to faith, not in a religious sense alone, but in the deep existential truth that to move forward requires stepping into uncertainty. He called this the leap of faith — the moment when logic and planning can take us no further when there is nothing left but the decision to step forward. Leadership, much like faith, is often about making choices without full certainty, trusting that meaning will emerge through action. There is no perfect data set, no absolute reassurance, only the willingness to begin. Leaders who cultivate hope do not wait for certainty before acting; they move toward the unknown, inviting others to do the same. Making a leap of faith need not be without supporting data, although this data may not come from your analytics team, but from your own gut.

Often dismissed as merely an organ of digestion, the gut possesses its own intelligence — a second brain known as the enteric nervous system, with over 500 million neurons — more than the spinal cord. Through the vagus nerve, it communicates constantly with the brain, shaping mood, intuition, and decision making, while the gut micro-biome produces neu-rotransmitters like serotonin, influencing anxiety and emotional regula-tion. This physiological network explains the experience of gut instinct — a knowing that emerges before conscious thought. Psychoanalysis and embodied cognition suggest that thought is not confined to the brain but extends into the body, aligning with ancient wisdom like the Japanese concept of hara as a centre of knowing. In leadership, paying attention to gut signals is not mysticism but intelligence — an awareness that decision making is as much a felt experience as a rational one. If anxiety lives in the body, so too does wisdom, reminding us that leading well is not only about thinking harder but about listening deeper to find the evidence that supports our leap of faith.

Faith was something that can be seen exhibited in Dante's Divine Comedy. In this epic poem, we go on a journey from despair to hope, from confusion to clarity, offering a powerful metaphor for leadership in times of uncertainty. The Divine Comedy, written by Dante Alighieri in the early 14th century, is an epic allegorical poem that follows the poet's journey through Hell, Purgatory, and Paradise, offering a profound meditation on sin, redemption, and the nature of the divine. At the poem's outset, Dante is lost in a dark wood, disorientated and unable to find his way. This mirrors the experience of a leader confronted by crisis, where the familiar terrain of certainty has vanished, and no clear path forward presents itself. His journey requires a descent into the Inferno, through the darkest aspects of the human psyche — sin, failure, and suffering — before he can ascend toward redemption and understanding.

Virgil, his guide through hell, represents reason and knowledge, but reason alone cannot carry Dante to the highest truth. As he moves through Purgatory and into Paradise, it is only through faith, love, and the guidance of Beatrice that he reaches the ultimate vision of light and meaning. Beatrice was Dante Alighieri's muse and idealised figure of divine love in The Divine Comedy. This progression suggests that intellectual analysis, while necessary, is not sufficient for true leadership; the capacity to hold vision, to sustain hope even when the path is unclear, is what ultimately enables transformation. The journey through the Inferno was not just about witnessing suffering — it was about understanding it, mining it for meaning, and making sense of what you might call the operating environment. The task of making sense of our circumstances, even when they might be unbearable, demands that we hold onto hope.

In the poem we see Dante as he moves through his testing circumstances, naming what he sees and confronting the consequences of human action. This act of seeing, of tolerating the darkness without succumbing to it, is essential in leadership. Those who avoid facing difficult truths often become trapped, unable to move forward. Dante was willing to navigate the depths without losing sight of the horizon; in this way he created his facilitating environment that allowed him to stay in touch with something hopeful. By the time Dante reaches the Paradiso, he is no longer the man who stood lost in the dark forest. His journey has reshaped him — not by avoiding suffering, nor by merely withstanding it, but by moving through it with hope. This reflects the challenge of leading through crisis: to step fully into complexity, to acknowledge struggle, yet to keep moving toward what lies beyond it. Hope, in this sense, is not blind optimism but an act of will, a commitment to the idea that meaning can be made even in the most uncertain of circumstances.

Key Takeaways

1. **The Importance of Being**
   Leadership isn't just about doing — it's about being. Creating space to think, staying present with uncertainty, and resisting the urge to jump to quick fixes makes for more thoughtful, sustainable leadership.

2. **Be Compassionate**
   Real compassion isn't about rushing in to fix things — it's about holding space for struggle. Leaders who acknowledge anxiety rather than push it away create a culture where people feel safe to think, act, and grow.

3. **Be Vulnerable**
   Dropping the mask of certainty makes leadership more human. When leaders show up as real people — not just as their role — it fosters trust, connection, and a shared sense of responsibility.

4. **Be Courageous**
   Courage isn't about fearlessness — it's about staying steady when uncertainty bites. Leaders who can hold their own anxiety, rather than spreading it, create a sense of stability for others.

5. **Be Creative**
   Innovation comes from tolerating not knowing for long enough. Instead of rushing for answers, creative leaders sit with uncertainty, allowing new ideas to take shape.

6. **Be Adaptive**
   Change is constant, and clinging to rigid plans only makes it harder. Adaptive leaders stay open, adjusting to what's emerging rather than forcing a pre-set direction.

7.   Be Hopeful

Hope isn't wishful thinking — it's about creating conditions where people can keep going. Leaders hold space for uncertainty while keeping the possibility of progress alive.

Chapter Five

Project Revisited

"We do not learn from experience... we learn from reflecting on experience."

John Dewey

The major project I referred to in the introduction of this book was notable not because of its scale, or complexity, or its success or failure. We completed the project on time and within budget, and after a few months of operation the government regulator judged it to be "safe." The operating model did increase demand dramatically, requiring resources that we simply didn't have. This design flaw ultimately meant the project was viewed as unsuccessful. However, what made this project important for me was the realisation that I was almost completely absent for the nine months it took to deliver. It was an activity that consumed my working day, every day, and I was obsessed with getting it over the line, yet I wasn't really there. It's only now that I can see how anxiety had completely taken control of me and was calling all the shots. Crucially, what I failed to notice at the time was how the anxiety of the group was affecting my emotional state, pulling me out of shape and off my leadership stance. I thought that the anxiety I was feeling was entirely mine and was something to be fought, pushed out of awareness and disavowed. In this assumption, I missed what might have been going on in the group, what the group was feeling, and how it was defending against difficult feelings associated with the reality of our predicament.

There was a clue, perhaps, in my initial sense of being a hero, chosen for a dangerous mission that only I could accomplish. This sense of inflation that we can sometimes get when we're told "you're special" is necessary. We humans need loving, affirming strokes from our parental figures from birth — if we are to survive. Research shows that human infants starved of affection will perish. Eric Berne[58], the founder of transactional analysis (TA), introduced the concept of 'strokes' to describe the ways we give and receive recognition in our interactions. These strokes play a crucial role in our psychological well-being and motivation. In essence, they shape how we feel seen and valued in our relationships. This need for external validation continues into adulthood, and work is a central place where we find it. Work is almost impossible if we don't receive feedback that we're OK. However, my experience at the time was hugely inflated; I felt joy at my colleague's apparent failure and an exaggerated sense of achievement at my selection for the role. My well-being was seemingly dependent on the endorsement I received from leaders. I was acting in service of a grandiose sense of self and had forgotten that I was just an ordinary leader, one member of a team. My relationship to the stroke had become distorted and unhealthy — I was being controlled by this want and had become needy.

My desire to maintain my specialness had become my priority and was interfering with my real priority of leading a project team. When this happens to leaders, our behaviour and communication shift from being in service of our task towards being in service of a hidden task: to uphold an illusion of who we think we are or what we think is going on. This illusion of being a heroic leader became more important to me than my actual leadership, and limited my capacity to mobilise the system to accomplish our goal. Thankfully, it wasn't constant; I would oscillate between being on-task and in service of my fantasy of specialness. I managed to move into an on-task mode just enough to deliver the project. In a sense, the part of me that was more grounded and wanted to be a rational leader won out in the end. To do so, I had to struggle with many other parts of myself that had different ideas. This anxious fight with myself was difficult and tiring, sapping me of the energy that would have been best used to think about what was needed.

As a child, I heard messages from authority figures that I was brilliant and also useless. This conflicting narrative set up what Bion called a valency that saw me accept the invitation to be a hero so enthusiastically. I needed to believe I was the hero. What I never noticed at the time was that the group of very powerful leaders that gave me this role also needed me to be the hero leader. Their anxiety meant they wanted to find a project leader with magical powers to save them from the terrible threat of failure. Their fantasy was that only a super-leader could relieve them of their anxiety. It allowed them not to look at all the data — to see reality with both my strengths and weaknesses. It also robbed them of the capacity to see their own strengths and weaknesses, and take up their roles based on a realistic appreciation of the task.

I took this fantasy of omnipotence into my team, where I quickly created a culture in which the talented people I worked with felt dependent on me for the answers. This wasn't a state that existed all the time and we were also able to create the conditions supporting cooperation and creativity. Two groups were present and, on occasion, work-group functioning emerged to accelerate our progress. However, my failure to listen and my tendency to put down others' suggestions resulted in a climate that was counter to our task. We had become what Bion described as a basic assumption dependency group, a group that worked under the unconscious assumption that a powerful leader would come up with a solution. This assumption blocked the creativity of others and disrupted our capacity to collaborate. Ultimately, I forced through delivery in a way that discounted the resources of other team members. If leadership is mobilising people to achieve a common goal, I was doing something else. I was defending against my anxiety of not being good enough by trying to be everything. I felt if I could just be the hero, then perhaps I would satisfy the voices inside me demanding the unattainable.

At the time of writing this book, I had coached and consulted to hundreds of leaders, as individuals and in groups, across a range of sectors and roles. Whilst I'm not keen on absolutes, it strikes me that the key developmental issue for the leaders I have worked with is a feeling of not being good enough. For some, this is obvious — they are in touch with it and can express what they feel readily. For others, it is an experience that is sublimated and denied. I sense that the idea that we are not enough is almost universal to the human experience, and it is an unstinting source of anxiety. I have linked this idea held within me to my need to be the hero leader, and banished the concept that I'm simply ordinary to the depths of my unconscious mind. Increasingly, I can see this feeling of not being enough as part of me — not the whole. It is as if there is an "I" that resides in me with other "I"s, some of which are friendly and others less so.

For me, the message "You're not enough" is teamed up with another: "You're not safe". These two ghouls haunted me to the extent that my task in life, and therefore work, had become "How do I silence these guys?" I initially attempted to do this not by exploring the reality of my situation, and finding data that might indicate my worth and safety (there was plenty of it if I had looked), but by investing in grandiose fantasies of omnipotence, and looking to authority figures to back this illusion up. This might explain why, when asked to write a business case that would both cast the net wider and reduce demand, I said yes. My fear of disappointing those in authority was so significant that I ignored the maths, and convinced myself that something impossible was possible. Some readers might put this down to an obvious incompetence and, of course, it was. However, given that I unconsciously believed my task to do something other than leadership — I was actually being very effective.

Interestingly, the board agreed with my proposal, despite the many assumptions on which it was built, and green-lighted the project with little deliberation. I remember thinking "that was easy"; wondering if my presentation of the project assumptions had landed, but not so much that I shouted about them until they noticed the assumptions would kill the project. I was relieved to be on the other side of the project design phase and keen to get stuck into practically doing. On reflection, I can see how the two powerful figures sponsoring this project felt impossible for me to challenge. They dominated the project board meetings, and the other members organised themselves around their take on events. They seemed to be doing all the work on behalf of the group. It was as if everything would be ok if only they kept talking. Often, it felt like the role of other board members was to listen to a comforting dialogue of organisational wisdom. This defence against anxiety was illustrated in Chapter Three in the description of basic assumption pairing. The unconscious assumption was that the pair would somehow produce a solution kept us trapped in an illusionary sense of hope. It is another way of avoiding the pain of reality, and organising around something made up that doesn't require the group to grow and develop.

If we had faced reality, we would have seen that creating a contact centre that had a greater scope, as the police desired, and reducing demand, as the council wanted, were goals in opposition to each other. The people leading this project were not incompetent — far from it — but they had chosen not to face the difficult aspects of their task. Perhaps this is what is meant by the expression "blind hope". In An Essay on Man, Alexander Pope wrote of humanity's tendency to "hope humbly" amidst chaos, encouraging balance between faith and rationality. Yet, in situations where hope becomes untethered from reality, it may become a form of self-deception — a refusal to confront the contradictions at hand. This suggests that blind hope can serve as a defence against facing uncomfortable truths, as was the case in this project. Instead of grappling with the inherent tensions, there was a persistent belief that somehow the contradictions could be reconciled simply by pressing forward with optimism. This way of being is not the same as being hopeful, a form of leadership promoted in the last chapter.

Just like the dependency culture I'd unknowingly created in my project delivery team, something similar was happening at board level. While this pairing was in play, real thinking, collaboration, and creativity just couldn't happen. The conditions of safety, of people feeling contained and safe enough to get it wrong or offer a dissenting voice, were absent. As a result, we found it relatively easy to sign off a business case based on numbers that simply didn't work. Our appreciation of reality was surrendered to blind hope. Looking back, I can see how both the head of the council and the head of the police service were under extreme pressure to pass regulatory inspections. They had both been told by their respective government regulators that the contact centre we were building was vital to the safety of vulnerable people in the county. It was as if they had also heard an unspoken message; that this project was also vital to their safety. I obviously know nothing of their inner worlds but can assume that they, like the rest of us, are subject to the normal range of human emotions. Perhaps these two leaders at the top of their organisations were ordinary like me, haunted by the same messages of not being good enough, of being out of their depth. I wonder if, in fact, three scared little boys were leading this project — each of us with an infantile part of ourselves emerging to take control of our leadership, and suppress our capacity to see things as they really were and face an unwelcome reality.

I can see now how the anxiety I felt throughout this project was a signal to me that I was blocking my leadership and allowing outdated parts of me to take control. It was just below the surface, slightly out of view, and I always knew that I was giving up on something — something was being sacrificed. That something was my own authority, my capacity to author my life — given away so as not to disappoint figures of authority, to maintain my status as a hero and stay safe. It was as if, despite my significant management responsibility and large salary, I felt like an imposter. I wasn't supposed to be there — I was meant to be driving a taxi on Great Yarmouth seafront. When we sacrifice something, we make it sacred. In sacrificing my personal authority, I made a sacred object of my learning.

This learning brought me to a difficult realisation: perhaps my anxiety, itself, had become a kind of defence. I had grown so accustomed to its presence that it had become a sort of refuge. Not a pleasant one, of course, but familiar. A place I could retreat to, steeped in self-pity and the narrative of failure. It was as if I were lying in a bath of my own shit — uncomfortable, fetid, but mine. Claimed. Known. Somehow, it affirmed me in my despair. Looking back, I wonder if the anxiety was shielding me from something even more painful. It may have been masking a deeper layer — an unacknowledged sadness, a quiet loneliness I couldn't quite face. And because those feelings were out of sight, I couldn't think about them or explore where they might have come from. When this happens, anxiety can take hold in a way that's both tormenting and oddly anchoring. We say we want rid of it and at the same time, we find it hard to let go. Because to do so means coming closer to the parts of ourselves we've disavowed.

One year after the project had ended my new boss looked up from his laptop to ask me those difficult questions I mentioned in the introduction. One question was: "Why didn't you manage up?" I obviously failed to convince in my response, and I wonder what might have happened if I was able to tell the story set out above. A story of how anxiety had engulfed me and the system in a way that distorted our sense of reality, and robbed us of the awareness needed to lead in uncertainty. It may not have mattered. I felt I had been nominated by the new turnaround leadership to be part of the problem. Someone had to be right. Otherwise, the system would have to reflect deeply on what had happened and how we were collectively responsible for what went wrong and, of course, what could be learned. We can often find it difficult to retain our own sense of goodness without locating our badness in another — something we do through projective processes that relieve us of difficult feelings and shield us from difficult questions. It's easier to say the old leaders were bad, and therefore not have to think about how it might be more complicated than that. It is so much harder for us to relate to each other and think together. I'm not arguing for never clearing out the leadership and sweeping with a new broom; this can be necessary. Doing so without thinking about what has gone before puts you at huge risk of repeating a systemic pattern that can function regardless of what personalities are in place.

Learning from this case study has meant I have had to reflect on the shadow aspects of my personality and therefore my leadership. When I asked the question "What went wrong?", the first answer that came is that I failed to effectively exercise my authority. What was needed, on reflection, was for me to say no. I knew the design of the target operating model was flawed and did push back a little, but when asked to go away and come up with a model that worked, I did so. Crucially, I retreated from the mathematics (the reality) and invested in the hypothetical model that the very smart analysts in my team had provided. I then lied to myself and believed that it would work, appending the assumptions to the business case. I made only a passing reference to them in my presentation. This self-deception was only just below the surface and helped me maintain an illusion of safety. The leaders I was reporting to represented authority figures from childhood in my mind. I wasn't aware of this at the time and I was, in fact, struggling with letting down a parental imago. The prospect of doing this was too terrible and it was avoided; I justified my actions and made one plus one equal three. If I could have seen what the project authority represented in my mind, perhaps I could have seen that I was acting in service of an archaic part of me that was no longer helpful.

Sublimating my personal authority was once useful. It was an adaption made to help me survive childhood. We all do it. This thing we call "I" is often a collection of adaptions employed to get us through childhood and into what some psychoanalysts call the 'first adulthood'. These adaptions are things like the need to please others, to be right, to be noticed, or to be loved. All of which feel familiar — if you'll excuse the pun — to me. It may be that we have adapted to our childhood circumstances by cultivating ambition and even a ruthless determination, or perhaps a sense of being a victim: that also comes with resentment and bitterness. These adaptions are not bad things, rather they are necessary for our psychological survival, needed to help us navigate the possibility of rejection and abandonment that accompanies our early years.

Unhelpfully perhaps, organisations are built along familiar lines. We build our organisations using the family as a template, in which leaders represent parents. This is unhelpful because this model is then perfectly designed to activate those outdated parts of us, which were once used as adaptions and now risk taking us back to an earlier stage of development. By the time we reach adulthood and even mid-life, the tapes we've been listening to since childhood have considerable momentum, becoming ever more amplified as they play on a continuous repeating loop. So much so that when we experience circumstances at work that unconsciously remind us of our early life, we regress to an infantile state of being. In this story, this is what happened to me. The authority figures at the project board represented my idea of authority, developed in childhood. This made it impossible for me to disappoint, lest their love be withheld. In my mind and many of our minds, such a withdrawal of approval is unconsciously experienced as annihilation. A psychological death too terrible for the nine-year-old boy residing in my psyche to bear. In those moments he took control and did what he had to do in order to survive.

Key Takeaways from Project Revisited

1. **Anxiety Warps Perspective**
   When anxiety goes unchecked, it distorts decision making. In this case, the leader absorbed the collective anxiety of the group, mistaking it as solely their own. This blurred their ability to step back and see the bigger picture.

2. **The Trap of Heroic Leadership**
   The fantasy of being the "chosen one" can be seductive, but it isolates. It offered temporary relief from uncertainty but ultimately led to exhaustion and a narrow view of leadership as a solo endeavour, rather than a collective task.

3. **Integrity Under Pressure**
   The tension between external expectations and inner truth creates deep unease. In this case, the leader knew the business case was flawed but felt compelled to push it through. The pressure to deliver clouded judgement and compromised integrity.

4. **The Power of Systemic Forces**
   Organisational pressures — shifting leadership, competing agendas, and unspoken expectations — shaped the project's course more than any individual decision. Yet, instead of recognising these as systemic, the leader personalised the burden.

5. **The Cost of Uncontained Anxiety**
   Running on adrenaline created an illusion of control, while eroding well-being. The emotional collapse while driving home was a wake-up call — anxiety had been steering the ship more than conscious choice. Seeking external support was a turning point.

6. **Resilience Isn't Enough**
   Completing the project didn't bring fulfilment, only exhaustion. Personal resilience alone wasn't sufficient — without structures

of support, leadership became an isolating, unsustainable effort.

7. **Anxiety as a Guide**

Over time, the experience reshaped the leader's relationship with anxiety. Rather than something to suppress, it became a source of insight — revealing hidden tensions, blind spots, and risks. Learning to listen to anxiety allowed for a more reflective, intentional leadership approach.

Chapter Six

Self-Leadership

"It is not what we achieve outwardly that will make us free, but what we do inwardly that will liberate us from fear."

James Hollis[59]

Self-Leadership

Because we learn early on that the safe response often involves denying the reality of our context and our feelings, we quickly organise ourselves in opposition to our own personal authority. In doing so, we estrange ourselves from ourselves; we eventually grow weary of the complexities of our personal history and, over time, we forget what matters most. This leaves us ill-equipped to author our own lives in- and outside work. Regaining this sense of personal authority is a central task of self-leadership, allowing us to lead with anxiety in every aspect of our lives. The work of self-leadership requires us to become self-aware, to reflect and notice. The more conscious we get, the more we can see the unconscious within us, and what it makes us do and stops us from doing. In this final chapter, we focus on how to cultivate the self-leadership necessary not just to transform our relationship with anxiety, but to transform anxiety into food for our growth as human beings.

Reflective Objects

It's said to be helpful for leaders to reflect and develop a habit of reflection. To think about events and consider why something is happening, its root causes, and its impact. Through self-reflection, we have more of a chance of successful self-leadership, rather than reflexively reacting to our emotions.

Academic Beverley Taylor[60] defines reflection as:

> "...the throwing back of thoughts and memories in cognitive acts such as thinking, contemplation, meditation, and any other form of attentive consideration in order to make sense of them, and to make contextually appropriate changes if they are required."

In physics, reflection refers to the "throwing back by a body or surface of light, heat, or sound without absorbing it". In both definitions, the words "throwing back" are used — perhaps no accident — the throwing back of thoughts and the throwing back of light, sound, or heat without absorption. It seems that reflection requires a reflective surface, a surface that can re-direct the energy. Following the spirit of this natural law, it is perhaps when thoughts are absorbed by a non-reflective surface that they are not thought about, and thinking doesn't take place. Perhaps our surface needs to be cleaned or polished to reflect effectively? But what exactly is it that needs to be polished? One way of thinking about this that has helped me is to view humans as spiritual beings — souls — and that the thing on the surface which can get in the way of reflection is our personality. In this sense, our souls are given to us; they represent the essence of who we really are, and our personalities are acquired, picked up along life's journey. When we try and reflect, we can get in our own way; ideas that we have about ourselves can block us from seeing things as they are. This might include an idea that we are always right, or more important than others. Or it may be that we see ourselves as "less than" and a victim. Both are forms of specialness that can obscure reality. Working on ourselves means seeing these objects that block reflection. For leaders to see the projections of others in a system, they need to be able to see their own projections, to be aware of how their personal history has affected their outlook, biases, and preferences.

If this is true, the task of leadership requires self-knowledge and an awareness of self that helps us see when our "stuff" is getting in the way of seeing things as they are. The thinking here points to the need to "work on your stuff"; the mental models, patterns of thinking, parental instructions, psychological complexes, scripts, and messages we pick up through life. Otherwise, your "stuff" will work on you! To do this means acquiring the capacity to see yourself as you really are. This work on self is akin to polishing the surface of your own lens, so that what is projected onto it is not obscured or absorbed. This idea certainly resonates with my experience; it was only when I was able to see how my lens was obscured by my defensive patterns, that I was more able to reflect on events in an organisational system.

Notes on Self

It was in 2016, right in the middle of the major project featured in the introduction and Chapter Five of this book, that I started a year-long therapy that changed everything. My therapist's approach was psychodynamic, and she helped connect my behaviour at work to my early experience in a way that felt helpful and healing. What felt most impactful was the invitation to reflect on myself, and it was then that I began to see that the main task of leadership was self-leadership. Leadership is clearly about mobilising people to achieve a goal, and it turns out that one's best chance at being successful at this is having the self-awareness to see when you are being managed by anxiety, instead of the other way around. Before starting this work with a therapist, I had already begun a practice of self-study. Specifically, I would write down observations noting my impressions of what was happening on the dance floor of the system I was working in, as well as events on my inner dance floor. From March 2011 to June 2020, I filled six little notebooks with what I called balcony observations — thousands of field notes recorded over almost a decade. In each little book I noted, often daily and sometimes hourly, observations of how I behaved and my impact on others. It was completing an executive education programme in adaptive leadership that prompted me to do this inner balcony work. Heifetz, Linsky, and Grashow[61] encouraged leaders to see themselves as a system, to understand what goes on emotionally under certain circumstances and adapt their leadership accordingly. I would notice reactions, feelings, emotions, and impressions and jot them down. I would often do this after a meeting and sometimes whilst in a meeting as the impression was being experienced. The practice became therapeutic itself and provided a huge amount of data for my coaching and therapy, and I continued doing it into my initial training at the Tavistock.

After just a few months of balcony observations, my notes began to tell a story. Years passed and I could identify entrenched patterns in how I was showing up as a leader. It was as if I was conducting a longitudinal study of "Garath Symonds", and the findings of this research project were beginning to emerge. The subject had some excellent leadership qualities; he was strategic, could think systemically and see the bigger picture, and was able to develop innovative plans with people. He could inspire others and could be kind, empathetic, and compassionate. There were, though, circumstances under which the subject reacted with anger and even aggressively with colleagues; he could interrupt people and talk over them. This sort of behaviour formed an obvious theme in the study, opening a significant line of inquiry. The patterns became obvious, and my notes on self were really an anxiety journal — it documented anxieties that were activated by the experience of leadership. The act of noting forced me to notice, facilitating that sideways step into a place in my mind from which I could observe myself. Viewing myself from the third position, I was able to gather data and discern these patterns of behaviour in a way that would not be possible when I was tangled up in the very events I was trying to observe. Perhaps this is what North American poet Walt Whitman meant when he talked of being "in and out of the game and watching and wondering at it" in his epic poem Leaves of Grass. Whitman often reflected on the idea of being both a participant in life and an observer, capturing the paradox of involvement and detachment. This quote speaks to the tension between engaging fully in life and taking a more reflective stance, watching events unfold from a distance.

Often, though, I was incapable of wondering at it; my persecutory superego would make the tyrannical assertion that I was at fault, wondering and reflecting were set aside in place of self-criticism and judgement. I tended to fall into a hole of regret and sadness where I would abide as a victim of my own experience. Wilfred Bion borrowed the term 'valency' from the natural sciences, to describe a psychological process whereby our behavioural tendencies bind with "objects" in our environment. In chemistry, the valency of an atom is a measure of its combining capacity with other atoms when it forms chemical compounds or molecules. Knowing and understanding your valencies is a crucial step in self-awareness. It allows you a greater capacity to notice when they turn up to run the show. By understanding their formation, you are better able to let them go, and to see your valency without becoming it. To do this requires self-study. Through my self-study, I noticed certain behavioural tendencies emerged under certain circumstances. I noticed a valency to feel inadequate in some way — not good enough and lacking.

At first, this was experienced simply as a feeling of anxiety, and on reflection, I noticed that certain situations — meetings, encounters, interactions — triggered this anxiety, and others did not. My problem was that the sorts of events that triggered my anxiety were those associated with the task of leadership. The more I recorded my impressions in my notebooks, the more clearly I could see a pattern that painted a picture of someone hyper-sensitive to criticism and judgement. Anxiety felt like the backdrop, an incessant white noise that was always there; when I saw a threat, I would react. It was as if the activity of leadership was divinely designed to make me anxious. And perhaps it was. Carl Jung[62] defined God in the following way:

To this day God is the name by which I designate all things which cross my wilful path violently and recklessly, all things which upset my subjective views, plans, and intentions, and change the course of my life for better or worse.

My reactions were always the same — I would attack. My way of defending against the anxiety I experienced was to be better, to argue; I could be aggressive and volatile, especially with those people I was supposed to be leading. This behaviour created a dissonance and eroded my personal authority. This part of me was a problem, and it didn't represent the whole; other aspects of my personality assisted my leadership and enabled some success. Sometimes success came because of my dissonant leadership style — I forced through results and was rewarded because of it. On other occasions, I managed to find the inner resources to lead with empathy and compassion.

The particular anxiety that evoked an authoritarian style of leadership in me was distinctly different from the anxiety we all feel in the face of life's normal uncertainties. It had its roots in my early childhood experience and loss. My self-study led me to the miserable and enlightening understanding that my personal history was having a significant influence over my leadership at work and in all other aspects of my life. When I was 14 years old my 12-year sister died in a road traffic accident. She was on her bike going to school when a van hit her and killed her. A year later, my mother and other sister and brother moved to London, and I stayed with my father. Not surprisingly, these events had a significant impact. The message I believe that I took in and swallowed whole at this time was that I was not safe and also not enough.

Later in life, I defended against the anxiety of not being enough by being defensive, combative, and argumentative, and was determined to succeed no matter what. My notes showed me that I would even argue in my mind with imaginary adversaries. Rehearsing was my manic defence against anxiety; I would repeatedly rehearse made-up situations in my head, portraying the psychology of someone under almost constant threat. This self-knowledge was helpful, and simply seeing it seemed to make it lessen. And it was also very unhelpful; there was a part of me that wished this knowledge had remained unconscious, unseen, and unavailable for examination. A part of me wished I was still asleep.

I saw things I didn't like, things that had perhaps always been there in plain view to others — but I'd never noticed them before. Unattractive and unwelcome opinions, traits, attitudes, and behaviours. This stuff belonged to me, and I denied it even after witnessing it from my inner balcony. More often than not, I would justify these behaviours, explaining them away as a consequence of my difficult circumstances, a by-product of being a senior leader in a complex organisation and my high-pressure role. Perhaps we all do that — write off behaviours that might otherwise be judged as harsh or inappropriate because we're special and we're doing a special job. This tendency to justify, explain, and excuse myself made my inner-balcony observations an intellectual activity — a fascinating exercise that eventually made me feel stuck, trapped in a pattern of behaviour that I couldn't escape. What was missing was the courage to see myself as I really was. With my childhood complexes in my way, my reflections on self and system as a leader were obscured, and my anxiety about not being enough or not being safe blocked my leadership.

Self-Observation and Self-Remembering

Somewhat by accident, I stumbled across the practice of self-observation. I asked my therapist a question that prompted a very strange answer. "Like what 'it' does not like," she said. This was strange because I didn't understand what she meant, and it was also the first time she had ever given me an instruction. It was from this point that the conversation took a dramatic turn, and our relationship shifted away from a conventional therapeutic contract. As it turned out, I was being offered a practice that would transform those difficult feelings my self-study had evoked into material that would feed my development. This practice was called self-observation, and it led me to eventually retire my notebooks to the shelf and instead start a new note of my impressions to be recorded in my body.

Later, when I studied systems-psychodynamics, I noticed how Ron Britton's[63] concept of the third position was like the practice of self-observation. Self-observation is about personal development; it's not about helping leaders understand their organisational system — it's about how humans can transform themselves. However, the link to the third position is the relationship between one's ability to be self-aware and one's capacity to reflect. When I started to try to "get up on the balcony" as a leader, and later to find a third position as a consultant-coach, I realised the benefit of having a self-observation practice first.

To know thyself is a fundamental spiritual teaching taught by all the great masters. Socrates taught it to his students, as did Krishna, Buddha, Lao Tzu, Jesus, and Rama[64]. One who engages in this inner work begins to throw light on the activities that take place within but are outside of ordinary consciousness. Special attention is necessary to see what goes on below the surface. This expression "below the surface" is used both in psychoanalytical and spiritual discourse, referring in both cases to something deep, perhaps buried, and out of our ordinary view. The "attention" needed to observe yourself must be cultivated by long practice; without it, we may never truly know ourselves psychologically. This blend of attention and observation makes all the difference, helping us learn from, and transform, our experience.

This ancient practice may also have a scientific grounding. German theoretical physicist Werner Heisenberg's Uncertainty Principle, is a cornerstone of quantum mechanics, suggesting that the very act of observing a particle changes its state. The more precisely we determine its position, the more its momentum becomes unknowable. This paradox reveals something profound — not just about physics but about leadership and self-awareness.

In leadership, as in quantum mechanics, observation is never neutral. The moment we turn our attention inward — to our motives, biases, or anxieties — something shifts. We are no longer simply doing, we are witnessing ourselves in the act of doing. Consider CEOs navigating a critical decision. If they operate purely on instinct, driven by habit and unexamined emotions, their choices may be swift but unconscious. However, if they engage in self-observation — pausing to notice their anxieties, impulses, and the subtle dynamics at play — their decision-making changes. Yet, paradoxically, the very act of observation alters what is being observed. The self they are examining is no longer the same self that was acting unconsciously a moment before.

This is the Leadership Uncertainty Principle: as we develop awareness, we cannot remain as we were, we cannot unknow what we now know. Leaders who cultivate deep self-observation will find their assumptions loosen, their presence deepen, and their ability to hold complexity expand. This is not passive introspection — it is an active engagement with the fluidity of self and system. This change doesn't happen quickly, and seeing ourselves without denial, justification, and avoidance can be painful. In his poem The Teaching, poet, author, and mechanic (of the human machine) Red Hawk[65] (Red Hawk is his given name; he is also known as Robert Moore) describes a teaching "as old as the stones". A teaching that came with humans to the earth. He describes the risks of self-observation and the possibility of confronting the horror of what you see. His advice is to do so without taking a personal interest or doing anything to change one's observations. We also need this capacity when observing organisational systems from the balcony, or the third position. For many, this practice will seem like mindfulness, and it is like mindfulness. It offers leaders a practical technique for achieving something akin to Freud's "evenly suspended attention"[66], a state of being that allows one's observation to cross the boundary into your inner world without interference.

The practice of self-observation requires you to find yourself, to locate yourself in time and space in the body. This management of the body is known as self-remembering; self-observation and self-remembering work as a single practice — they are one thing. The fundamental principles that guide this practice are explained in Red Hawk's 2009 book: Self-Observation – The Awakening of Conscience: An Owner's Manual. Since I started my practice of self-observation in 2017, I've read this book around eight times; I always return to it and always will. Below, I've described my own experience of self-observation, attempting to link it to systems-psychodynamic thinking. I highly recommend you read Red Hawk's book yourself before developing your own practice.

My Practice

Not judging your impressions, thoughts, feelings, and sensations isn't easy, and it's the start of the process of self-observation. When one starts to watch one's mind, this becomes obvious as it seems like the mind is mechanically sorting everything into good and bad, like and dislike, almost as if this were its primary task — the task it must accomplish to survive. We seem to be endlessly comparing and labelling our experience in a way that often provokes anxiety. This trait seems similar to the splitting into good and bad parts in object-relations theory, central to Klein's idea of projective identification. This is the sort of black-and-white, concrete thinking we have as children, or on those occasions in adulthood when we slip back into an earlier stage of development.

Scottish neurologist and psychiatrist Maurice Nicholl advised the practitioner of self-observation to separate themselves into two — the observer and the experience, or that which is being observed. This splitting reminds me of Britton's[67] place in the mind where we can step sideways to observe and imagine ourselves being observed. The difference made by splitting yourself in this way can be seen by how we frame our experiences. In this process you create a space between you and your experience; your experience and your identity are no longer entangled.

Nicholl, like Wilfred Bion, was a First World War army officer; he later went on to work with Carl Jung[68] before studying a spiritual tradition known as the Fourth Way with its founders G.I Gurdjieff and P.D. Ouspensky[69]. The experience of war had a dramatic impact on both men, and perhaps their outlook, from then on. Could violent conflict make Nicholl and Bion's own anxiety become such a primary concern that they committed to investigating this phenomenon so deeply? Nicholl offered the aphorism "this is not 'I'" as a way of remembering ourselves when we get tangled up with our experience — a shock to the system that allows us to put some space between the observer and what is observed. In this effort to split yourself, the intention is not to change what you observe but rather not to be it: If I see it, I don't have to be it.

My experience of self-observation was that it started as enlightening and quite soon became a maddening mental torture. It was when I failed to not judge it, when I identified with my experience, that I felt the pain of self-observation that Red Hawk[70] warns against in his poem The Teaching. I saw myself as I really was without a buffer; I was horrified by what I was witnessing, unequipped to deal with this revelation. All the ideas I had about myself and how I reflexively protected myself against them were revealed. These adaptions had momentum, decades of energy behind them, compelling me to live my life mechanically — a life during which, more often than not, my anxiety-fuelled adaptions were in control.

Luckily, I had some invisible help; my breath and also my bodily sensation were always there for me. Irish author, poet, and philosopher John O'Donohue[71] talked about the idea of invisible help in the Celtic spiritual tradition. It's funny how you can see it when you have eyes to see. Something I could see and spent most of my life ignoring became a source of help; it took my observations from my head into my heart and hand. Self-observation is not enough; the deployment of attention on bodily sensation and a relaxed body is required to make the practice whole[72]. This practice of bodily sensation is called self-remembering. By switching the attention away from the intellectual centre into the body, we place our attention in the here and now, in the present moment. It is by working with this intelligence centred in the body that our observations are recorded in the body; it was doing this that allowed me to retire my notebooks.

This practice means we don't get captured by our habitual thought patterns that automatically start working if we don't watch them. Red Hawk[73] describes these practices as the first three laws of self-observation:

1. Self-observation without judgement.
2. Don't change what is observed.
3. No observation without sensation.

In his little manual, Red Hawk describes self-remembering as an instrument of transformation, telling us how what he calls coarse materials — emotions like anxiety — that enter the body are transmuted or converted into finer material, namely love. In this sense, the body is a piece of apparatus that allows us to transform our emotions from something painful to something that is nurturing and supportive. In this spiritual or esoteric tradition, our painful and difficult emotions are often described as food to be metabolised by the body through the process of self-remembering. This is illustrated in what is viewed as the higher meaning of the line from the Lord's Prayer "Give us this day our daily bread"; a request for "food", and a daily conscious commitment to remember ourselves.

When we consider this progression as a system or process, it is as if our negative emotions — or coarse energies — in the form of rage, anxiety, hate, depression, and anger are imported into the body, where they undergo a conversion process and are metabolised into finer energy or love. In other words, love is the output of the system. In this understanding, the body is an instrument of transformation that converts coarse energy into higher energy for our growth and development as human beings. Self-remembering is the process of converting emotions like anxiety into something useful — love.

Self-Leadership: Pause, Remember, Love

The pause, think, act method described previously offers a technique for leaders to reorientate themselves to anxiety: the anxiety that is activated by circumstances that relate to our personal history, the anxiety that is projected into us by the group, and the anxiety that we introject that is a reaction to our uncertain context. The invitation was to pause and create a containing third space in which reverie can take place, as the leader contains the anxieties of others. In this model, the focus is self-leadership and the thinking is replaced by a process of self-remembering, where our emotions are transformed by the body and the output of this transformation is love.

Figure Four

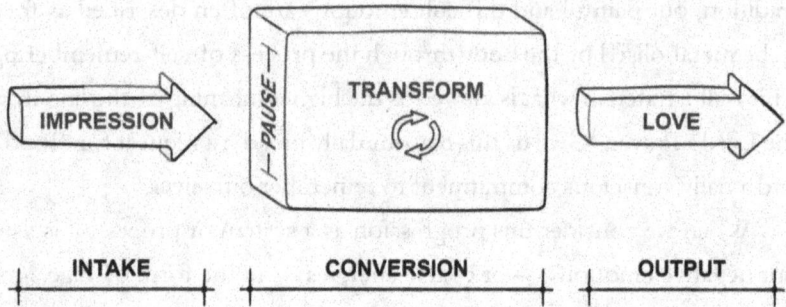

Remembering

An impression is experiencing an emotion, feeling, or sensation. Imagine the impression of anxiety; it is felt in the body, and you pause to notice it. Taking this impression into your system, you place your attention on your bodily sensation, sensing into what it feels like to be in a body. Sensing is something to be practised. It involves feeling your bodily vibration, your blood flowing, your breath, and your heart beating. Sensing makes you more sensitive, as you even imagine the molecules and atoms you are made of. Physicists tell us that everything in the universe is made of energy, reconnecting with this idea is an act of self-remembering. The output of the process is love. There is no thinking involved as the body knows what to do — it always has.

In discovering Bion's description of maternal reverie, I noticed some striking similarities with self-remembering, even down to the use of words like "instrument" and "metabolise". For Bion[74], this purpose of the psyche can be related to a digestive model of the workings of the thought-thinking apparatus. At the beginning of its life, the infant does not have access to a thought-thinking apparatus that is mature enough to use and integrate its very first mental and emotional experiences. Bion called these unbearable thoughts and emotions 'beta elements' — emotional states linked to the infant's very earliest sensory and relational experiences. Unable to process these beta elements themselves, they project them into the mother, who, through her capacity for maternal reverie, transforms them into what Bion called 'alpha elements'. In this way, the mother modifies the child's experiences. She helps them process their experience, returning the feelings to the child in a form that is digestible through what's called re-introjection.

The thinking is that this seemingly "far out" technique is vital for human development and maturation. Reverie and self-remembering look like the same — or very similar — processes. One is practised by an individual to grow and mature as a human being, and the other by a mother to help her child grow and mature vicariously through her. In this sense, children may experience self-remembering in infancy, as mothers instinctively perform this ancient practice of human development. It's only after collecting a lifetime of experience that this practice is needed once again — when the joy of childhood has receded to leave a personal history that needs our attention. In giving ourselves attention in this way we develop as human being and as leaders, growing in our capacity to regulate our emotions and be in the uncertainties of organisational life.

Central to the idea of self-remembering is the notion that we are identified with objects (to use a Kleinian[75] expression) that are not us. This means our identity — or who we think we are — and the object become the same thing. This idea is seen when we say or think "I am anxious", rather than "I am experiencing some anxiety". In this shift or turn, we create the space to think from the third position, and this illuminates the source of the problem: you are identified with being something that you are not. In other words, in these moments of identification, we forget who we really are. This, of course, invites the question: "Who am I?"

From the perspective of the many transpersonal or spiritual traditions, the answer to this question is that we are that which is aware of our experience. If you can observe your anxiety objectively without judgement, your relationship to the object changes, and you become the observer of anxiety and are no longer anxious. At least that's the theory, and achieving this state of being takes practice; I believe that's why it's called spiritual practice. When we witness our emotions, we then don't have to attribute them to someone else; we don't have to deny, split, and project in the way described by Melanie Klein[76] in her explanation of projective identification.

Answering the question "who am I?" beyond being aware of your experience is a task best left to others more expert on this subject. It seems to me, though, that if we are not our various objects of identification, or in other words, if we are not a thing, we are then no-thing. To remember yourself means to remember who you really are, which requires a surrender into no-thingness. Being nothing isn't necessarily an attractive proposition; indeed, calling someone nothing is often used as an insult. This idea infers that what is real about us is not our experience or our body or material possessions — not even the thing we call our lives — but rather our awareness of our life. The emphasis here is that we are no-thing, and as such, we are everything, one with all that is, made of the same energy as the entire cosmos. This state of development or self-remembering, where you identify with being the awareness of experience rather than experience, is advanced, and for most of us one we only glimpse in rare moments of consciousness. That's not to say we shouldn't strive to achieve this state, if only we can remember to do so.

Cultivating Stillness

To close your eyes in meditation is an act of courage. It involves being with ourselves alone, being in our inner world undistracted by experience. Many will tell you that they've tried meditation and it's not for them; "I don't have the patience" they'll tell you. The word patience originates from the Latin patientia, meaning "suffering, endurance, submission", which itself comes from pati, meaning "to suffer" or "to endure". So, at its core, patience is deeply tied to the idea of bearing, enduring, and suffering, but over time it has evolved to also signify self-restraint, calmness, and perseverance. It's worth thinking that when we say we don't have the patience for medita-tion, what is it that we are unable to endure? It may be that what's needed when we meditate is the ability to endure the pain of being in our inner world, where we are exposed to the psyche's agenda without protection. Confronting the contents of our inner world isn't easy, and learning to be with ourselves — all of ourselves — is a crucial step in changing our relationship with anxiety.

Blaise Pascal, the French mathematician, physicist, and philosopher ob-served this in 1670 when he said:

> "All of humanity's problems stem from man's inability to
> sit quietly in a room alone."

In a sense, Pascal is suggesting that distraction is a defence against anxiety. In the constant rush of corporate life, where leaders are expected to be in perpetual motion, the art of solitude is often lost. Yet it is precisely in stillness, when the distractions fall away, that true insight emerges. Many leaders resist solitude because it forces them to confront their thoughts, doubts, and fears. Pascal understood this, identifying that much of human behaviour is driven by the need to escape the discomfort of our inner world. Leaders often follow this same pattern. Meetings, endless tasks, and immediate responses can defend against the vulnerability of uncertainty. Relentless busyness has become a common social defence against anxiety; what better reason not to exercise authority, not be on-task, and to avoid taking responsibility for a dysfunctional culture, than "we're too busy"?

The challenge that Pascal issued centuries ago is no less urgent today. It is not a call for withdrawal but an invitation to engage the world with more clarity and purpose. Leaders who can sit with discomfort, rather than fleeing it, come to embody a different kind of authority — one grounded in wisdom rather than reactivity. Creating stillness, for yourself, your group or team, and the entire organisation is foundational to creating the containment necessary to pause in a way that enables thinking.

Meditation can also be a process of connecting with something higher than us, something that nourishes the soul and soothes the mind. The focus on the here and now helps us find some relief from the past and future, and the regret and anxiety that it can bring with it. In this task, we are provided with amazing tools — our bodily sensations and breath. Our capacity to pause and avoid reflexively reacting to our outer circumstances is an almost impossible task, made possible by self-observation. A meditation or sitting practice can prime us for this work in the moment; it's like a daily exercise routine that makes the pause more possible. Sitting in the morning and again at night before going to bed is ideal. In this way, we bookend our day and ground ourselves in the present, to prepare us better to receive impressions throughout our day.

Practical Ways to Integrate Solitude

1. Structured Reflection

Create deliberate time to step away from external demands. This might mean a quiet hour in the morning, journaling, or simply sitting in stillness without a device or agenda.

2. **Walking Without Input**

   Instead of filling every walk with podcasts or calls, allow the mind to wander. Insights often emerge in unstructured mental space.

3. **Decision Making Through Stillness**

   Before major decisions, take time to sit with the question rather than rush to an answer. What emerges in the quiet is often more profound than what is found in immediate discussion.

4. **Holding Organisational Stillness**

   Encourage space for reflection within teams. Not every moment needs to be filled with action; sometimes the most valuable leadership move is to allow silence and let thoughts surface organically. Try a "mindful minute" before meetings start, even between each agenda item, as a way of cultivating team stillness.

The Work

The work of self-leadership is most obviously about embarking on, and continually returning to, a path of self-knowledge. This path must be returned to because it is so very easy to come off it and lose your way, in an unconscious effort to avoid your reality. This work is assisted by self-observation, allowing the practitioner to see their habits, patterns, and reflexive adaptions in a way that was previously not possible. A by-product of this new awareness is the horror of seeing yourself without the buffer of your personality in the way. This is why the practice needs to be done with impartiality, a non-judgemental stance that allows you to see yourself as you are and not as you imagine you are. As already mentioned, this is no easy thing to do, and this awareness can even make you hate what you see and observe. I'm aware that the idea of self-hatred has not had much coverage in the leadership and management body of knowledge. And the message "I hate myself" may be one that torments many of us, even leaders. How to orientate to this request takes work; work that puts you in the right relationship with yourself and puts your anxiety into context. Growing in self-knowledge allows you to see what's yours, to see your projections and the material from your personal history. Doing this, you are better equipped to discern when the anxiety you are feeling belongs to the group or the wider system.

Hatred of self may not be something that we consciously think about, and it might be what is behind the sense of not being enough or the imposter syndrome that affects so many of us in leadership roles — perhaps even to the extent that our whole career becomes a lifelong project to be accepted and loved by the group. The maleficent presence of hatred is why the instruction to observe yourself is given to do so without judgement, to accept what you see regardless of how repellent some parts of the contents of our unconscious are. This is an invitation to love all of yourself, the good bits and the bad. Failing to do so will mean those so-called "bad bits" show up later as unexpected and unwelcome guests. Our efforts to avoid the contents of the psyche, or our soul, is ultimately fruitless, as the soul has its own way of catching up with us.

Presenting meditation and mindfulness as an important tool in leadership has been done by many, and whilst important, it may not be enough on its own. Self-observation is necessary to acquire the self-awareness necessary to lead our self, and self-remembering is vital to transform our experience. Ultimately, this involves what John O'Donohue[77] called "the beautiful, but difficult, spiritual work of learning to love yourself." It's difficult because it means an authentic encounter with yourself. Carl Jung[78] in *Modern Man in Search of a Soul* put it like this: "The most terrifying thing is to accept oneself completely." This difficult lifelong practice is perhaps the single most effective way of making the source of our anxiety visible, and not a dreadful unseen ghost.

The Meaning of Anxiety

In my personal and professional experience, two perspectives have profoundly shifted my relationship with anxiety: the systemic and psychodynamic insights from the Tavistock tradition, and the transpersonal teachings of the Fourth Way. These frameworks have taught me that anxiety can serve not as a disabling weight, but as a resource — something that informs leadership and nurtures human development. For much of my life, anxiety felt meaningless — a harbinger of weakness or an amorphous dread that defied explanation. It was something to avoid or endure and, admittedly, sometimes still is. What I am learning to do, however, is change my relationship with this pervasive feeling. Rather than treating anxiety as a flaw to be remedied, I am learning to see it as an integral and even essential part of the human experience

Becoming Human: A Leadership Imperative

An executive coach I was working with whilst I was in a leadership role, once said to me that personal development and leadership development are the same thing. At the time I wasn't sure of this, believing that to be a better leader I needed to go to Harvard or Judge and acquire lots of knowledge about leadership as a concept. It took me a while and I began to understand that acquiring knowledge was crucial, not from books or management gurus, but from studying myself. I realised what my coach meant was that I had to become a better person — a better human being — if I wished to develop as a leader. In other words:

"Becoming a real human being really is the primary leadership issue of our time... If you want to be a leader, you have to be a real human being. You must recognise the true meaning of life before you become a great leader. You must understand yourself first." (Chinese Confucian philosophy — 551-479 BCE).

When I first discovered the quote above, I thought "that's really true". Not noticing that it was ancient wisdom, I thought it was written about our time — the 21st Century! Realising that it was said around 2500 years ago stunned me, as developing our humanity remains the primary leadership issue of our time. How to become a "real human" remained puzzling to me. Sigmund Freud once described anxiety as "a riddle whose solution would be bound to throw a flood of light on our whole mental existence." In wrestling with the nature of anxiety, Freud believed we could unlock fundamental truths about the human mind. It seems plausible that Freud's metaphor of light referred to the light of awareness — our ability to direct attention inward, to observe our experience without distortion, and to uncover deeper truths.

For leaders, the challenge extends beyond personal understanding. They must grapple with the anxiety not only of the self but also of the groups and organisations they lead. The concept of projective identification reminds us that the emotions we carry may not entirely be our own. Leaders, then, face the formidable task of making sense of not just their anxiety but also the collective anxieties projected onto them by others.

Three Essential Self-Leadership Tasks

In navigating anxiety, leaders can benefit from focusing on three interrelated tasks of self-leadership:

1. Containing and Making Sense of One's Own Anxiety

The first task is not to be overwhelmed by anxiety but to hold one's ground without denying or suppressing the experience. This entails courage — a courage not to do but to be in the midst of discomfort. Plato described this as courage in the face of danger — not the bravery of action, but the resilience to endure without being consumed by fear. By containing anxiety and resisting automatic reactions, leaders open the possibility for reflection. To achieve this, they must cultivate a 'third position' — an objective stance from which they can observe both external events and their internal reactions, gaining insight into what the anxiety is signalling.

2. Transforming Anxiety

The final task is to use anxiety as a catalyst for growth. By remembering oneself — remaining aware of one's thoughts and sensations without being overtaken by them — it becomes possible to transform raw emotion into something more refined and purposeful. This process involves what the Fourth Way teachings refer to as 'intentional suffering': consciously bearing discomfort to transcend habitual reactions and allow for personal evolution. Anxiety, when reorientated in this way, becomes nourishment for the development of the self.

3. Get Help

Developing self-leadership involves self-reflection and introspection, but relying solely on your own personal resources can be difficult. It is important, perhaps even necessary, to get help with this task. The idea that personal development and leadership development are the same thing, as referred to earlier, is an idea that I only agree with partially, as it ignores the effects of the group and the possibility of projective identification. However, it's vital that we work on ourselves and develop the self-awareness to allow us to lead in a way that is not impeded by our personal history, childhood messages, complexes, scripts, and adaptions. This work can be assisted enormously by self-study, self-observation, and self-remembering, and finding someone to help you makes all the difference. Personal therapy, counselling, and coaching that uses a psychologically informed approach are excellent sources of help. Groups are also very helpful, especially when they are facilitated by someone trained in group work. Ironically perhaps, self-leadership is something we shouldn't do alone; it's too important a task to take on without someone who can act as a mirror, sensitively and compassionately helping us to see what we are blind to.

Anxiety as an Invitation

The three tasks described above are presented as distinct steps but often occur simultaneously. When head, heart, and hand align, anxiety shifts from being a debilitating force to a vital data point, offering valuable insights into oneself and the system in which one operates. It invites leaders to embody compassion — toward themselves and others — and to engage with life's uncertainties as opportunities for growth.

In Buddhism, the Bodhisattva is a spiritual warrior driven by a desire for truth, who willingly turns toward pain rather than fleeing from it. Buddhist nun Pema Chödrön teaches that we must explore the turbulence and unpredictability of life rather than push it away. She describes the experience of being caught in the "chain reaction of reactivity", and the importance of pausing to observe.

Instead of criticising ourselves or succumbing to shame, she urges us to:

> "Just feel the rage, feel the shame, feel the guilt, feel the
> remorse, feel the heat, feel the fire — just as it is, just as
> it is…"

This act of conscious suffering — bearing our emotions without flinching — allows for transformation. For Chödrön, this is where genuine growth occurs.

Carl Jung[79] emphasised that not all suffering is the same. There is a distinction between authentic suffering, which leads to insight and healing, and inauthentic suffering, which perpetuates patterns of avoidance and denial. Similarly, the Fourth Way teachings invite us to suffer intentionally — to endure discomfort to awaken and shed patterns that no longer serve us. Like the Bodhisattva, this path requires the courage to "sit in the fire" as the outdated and unhelpful parts of ourselves burn away. Just as anxiety once acted as an early-warning system alerting us to predators, it can now serve as a reminder to wake up — to become present to our own inner state. In this way, it prompts us to take responsibility for our emotions and respond consciously, rather than reacting automatically.

The 13th-century Sufi poet Rumi[80] beautifully illustrates this in his poem The Guest House:

> "This being human is a guest house. Every morning a
> new arrival. A joy, a depression, a meanness, some mo-
> mentary awareness comes as an unexpected visitor."

Rumi invites us to welcome all emotions as honoured guests, even those that disturb our peace:

> "The dark thought, the shame, the malice, meet them at
> the door laughing, and invite them in."

This metaphor encourages us to create a space between ourselves and our experience — to greet our feelings with curiosity and acceptance rather than resistance. By doing so, we open ourselves to the possibility of learning from our emotional experiences.

> "Be grateful for whoever comes, because each has been
> sent as a guide from beyond[81]."

The Courage to Be

The willingness to fully experience our emotions shows a particular kind of courage — not the grit of physical endurance, but the quiet bravery of surrender. Paul Tillich[82] described this as "the courage to be", the existential resolve to live authentically despite the inevitability of death. Tillich saw anxiety as the awareness of our mortality — a confrontation with the boundary of existence itself. In systems-psychodynamic terms, this boundary represents the ultimate threat of annihilation. Kleinians[83] argue that struggles with mortality in adulthood often echo early infantile anxieties. If an individual remains fixated on the danger out there, death may be experienced as an external persecutor, leading to rigid defences such as denial or projection. If they can engage from a more reflective position, they are more able to integrate the reality of death, mourning the inevitable losses of life while continuing to engage with the world in a meaningful way. We don't need to think about our actual passing for this unconscious process to be doing its work of making us anxious. It persists throughout life as something unthought and unconsidered, a quiet protest in the face of non-being.

However, if the evitability of death puts us in touch with anxiety, perhaps anxiety also reminds us that we are alive — no longer infants dependent on the embrace of a caregiver, but adults capable of self-awareness and resilience. In these moments, leadership grounded in courage and self-awareness emerges — not supported by the reassuring embrace of another, but by our capacity to be in the world despite our anxieties. In this way, anxiety becomes not a force to be feared, but a call to presence — a reminder of our humanity and an invitation to step forward as real human beings. This idea of finding the courage to be despite anxiety strikes me to be at the core of our task when leading with anxiety. It was on those occasions when anxiety was calling the shots that I needed this courage the most.

These were the times when my leadership was in service of defending against my anxiety, of maintaining a fantasy that I was in control, or justifying not doing what needed to be done. On occasions I found an aggression, a determination to push through in the face of anxiety, and this was not conscious action — my view still obscured, and my leadership still shackled to the idea of self-preservation. I found meaning in being right, success, and narcissistic endorsement. The roots of my anxiety turned out to be related to a feeling of not being safe, and not good enough. My fears of rejection and abandonment feel so very connected to my relationship with authority, a parental imago, which showed up throughout my leadership career in the authority figures with whom I worked. Klein[84] argued that the infant projects this instinct outward, experiencing the world as hostile and persecutory. This leads to what she called persecutory anxiety, a primitive form of fear that shapes early object relations and can continue into adulthood as a shadow of something that remains unresolved.

I have learned that this anxiety can be worked through. It involves us tracking back through the uncertain fog to the fear we know but can't think about — coming to terms with what was, and seeing that the past doesn't have to determine the future. This process leaves us with what remains —

normal anxiety — about our performance in life and work, and its impact on us and the world. This form of anxiety is not wrapped in a neurosis or a childhood complex but is rather the healthy life-affirming signal that there is an unknown danger out there and you need to pay attention. This is the nature of the anxiety that remains when we can see things as they are, and not as we imagine them to be, giving in to our sense of fantasy, or seduced by the anxiety of the group. To do this requires us to find a reflective mode of functioning that embraces the and bothness of our circumstances. "And both" means accepting both the good and the bad and integrating the two. Work and life are both difficult and joyful. This relationship with anxiety means being able to hold the good and the bad at the same time.

This change in our relationship to anxiety means changing our relationship to life. It asks us to step beyond the habitual defences that shield us from discomfort and to stand, fully present, in the truth of our existence. To walk around like vulnerable knights, without our armour. To welcome our experience, as Rumi suggests in The Guest House[85], is not to revel in suffering but to recognise that each feeling, no matter how unwelcome, carries an invitation — to learn, to integrate, to become more fully ourselves. Anxiety, when not distorted by old ghosts or collective panic, is simply a signal, a pulse of awareness that we are alive and that something important is at stake. The realisation that I am an anxious leader invited me to make meaning of my experience in a way that was previously too difficult. I began to see that the determination and drive to perform that got me through the first half of life was a way of not facing the impact of my personal history. Seeing my habits and patterns, what they made me do and stopped me from doing, was a terrible gift, and something I would choose every time over the unknown horror of anxiety. To receive this gift, I had to lead interiorly, not from a place of certainty but from a place of grace. It may be that is what leadership truly is — the willingness to stand in the unknown, not paralysed by what might be lost, but moved by what still remains to be discovered. It's a task that we must continually return to, endeavouring not to absent ourselves even for a single breath.

Final Takeaways

1. **Anxiety is Data**

   Anxiety is not an obstacle but a guide — it reveals what is unspoken in the system. Leaders who listen to their anxiety, rather than suppress it, gain insight into what needs attention.

2. **Leadership is Contagious**

   Those around them absorb a leader's emotional state. Anxiety spreads, but so does clarity, containment, and thoughtfulness. The choice is yours.

3. **Defences Block Thinking**

   When anxiety is overwhelming, leaders resort to blame, avoidance, or rigid control. These defences feel protective but ultimately weaken leadership by shutting down learning and connection.

4. **Uncertainty is Inevitable — Your Response is a Choice**

   Leadership will always involve ambiguity and pressure. The question is not how to eliminate uncertainty, but how to hold steady and think in its midst.

5. **The Work is Never Done**

   Awareness of anxiety is not a final achievement but an ongoing practice. Leadership requires continuous reflection — on yourself, your team, and the system you are shaping.

Acknowledgements

This book emerged from a life-changing educational experience: training in systems-psychodynamic consulting at the Tavistock & Portman NHS Trust. I am deeply indebted to the faculty and staff of the programme known as the D10. My gratitude extends to the course leaders, Kay Trainor and Gwen Hanrahan, and all the tutors, teachers, experiential leads, observation leads, and administrators who so skilfully curated this learning journey. The support of my supervisor, Miranda Alcock, profoundly enriched the experience. Her brilliance and expert guidance allowed me to join the dots between theory, practice, and my personal history — what might otherwise have been a confusing or even maddening task. I would especially like to thank the students of the ED10/D10 class of 2024. It was the group that made the learning possible. The challenge, support, love, laughter, anxiety, and hate we experienced together shaped us. I am grateful to this group of brilliant people and feel honoured to have journeyed alongside each of them.

It took two decades of leadership to prepare me for what I learned at the Tavi. During those years in leadership roles, there were times when I was authentically engaged in the activity of leadership, and times when I was doing something else entirely. That something else was often in service of defending against my own anxiety, reflexively reacting to events linked to my personal history. I remain grateful to all those I worked with throughout my career for the learning, patience, and grace you offered me. It perhaps goes without saying that if I knew then what I know now, I would have done it differently. My thanks go also to those that kindly and perhaps stoically read my early drafts and generously gave me feedback: Dil Sidhu, Lucy McGrath, Victoria Phillips, Phil Edelston, Charlotte Best, Nula Cooper, and Rach Masters. Special thanks to Dr Sarah Hughes for writing such a thoughtful and considered foreword. Thanks also to Nicole Rowntree, the brilliant artist who generously allowed me to use her work for the cover of the book.

Finding the path of personal development would not have been possible without the support of two remarkable women: Sarah Willis and Josie Gregory. Sarah was my coach for nearly eight years. With her support, I began to see myself as I am. Josie, the therapist referred to throughout this book, introduced me to the practice of self-observation. It is this practice that helps me do something productive with my new awareness. I will always be deeply grateful to these two expert practitioners for their insight and compassion, as I wrestled with the task of leadership and struggled with myself. I owe heartfelt thanks to my colleagues, mentors, and friends; those who stood beside me in consultancy rooms, at the edge of difficult group conversations, and on long mountain walks where ideas slowly found form. Your presence, your honesty, and your willingness to think with me have shaped every page of this book. On a more personal level, I want to thank the writers who have helped me connect with the deeper currents within. James Hollis, whose Jungian reflections have been a source of fierce clarity; and Red Hawk, whose poetry and instruction in self-observation has helped me attend to the inner life with tenderness and precision. Their books are worn and weathered now; underlined, dog-eared, and sacred to me through use.

Above all, I want to thank my family, Sarah, Tom, and Joseph. Leaving a corporate career to become a consultant, undertake a master's, and write a book would not have been possible without their love. This book is dedicated to them.

Lastly, I must thank the mountains of Eryri, North Wales, a place that contained me and helped me think throughout this process.

Credit for cover art

Original cover artwork by Nicole Rowntree.
www.nicolerowntree.com

About the Author

Garath Symonds is a leadership adviser, organisational consultant and executive coach. Earlier in his career, he held senior roles in the public sector. Those years shaped his curiosity about what really goes on beneath the surface of leadership, especially how anxiety affects the way people relate, decide and lead. In time, that curiosity led him to retrain at the Tavistock Centre, where he studied systemic and psychodynamic approaches to leading and consulting. His work now focuses on the often-unseen dynamics that shape organisational life, how leaders carry anxiety, the roles they're drawn into, and the group processes that can help or hinder them. Away from consulting, Garath turns to nature and walking in the wild places of Britian as a source of wellbeing and inspiration.

Contact: garath@spacetoreconnect.com

Notes

1   Alain de Botton, "Quote on Anxiety," Goodreads, accessed February 4, 2025, https://www.goodreads.com/quotes/12345-despite-its-maddeningly-vague-inarticulate-form-anxiety-is-almost.

2   Rollo May, The Meaning of Anxiety (New York: Ronald Press, 1950).

3   Melanie Klein, "Notes on Some Schizoid Mechanisms," The Journal of Psychotherapy Practice and Research 5 (Spring 1946): 160–179.

4   Ibid.

5   Rollo May, The Meaning of Anxiety (New York: Ronald Press, 1950).

6   Søren Kierkegaard, The Concept of Anxiety (Copenhagen: Reitzel, 1844).

7   Paul Tillich, The Courage to Be, 2nd ed. (New Haven: Yale University Press, 2000; first published 1952).

8   Ibid.

9   Kurt Lewin, Field Theory in Social Science: Selected Theoretical Papers, ed. Dorwin Cartwright (New York: Harper & Row, 1951), 240.

10 Kurt Lewin. "Frontiers in Group Dynamics: Concept, Method and Reality in Social Science; Social Equilibria and Social Change." Human Relations 1, no. 1 (1947): 5–41.

11 Tracy Vannorsdall, "COVID-19 and Anxiety," Johns Hopkins Medicine, accessed November 17, 2023, https://www.hopkinsmedicine.org/health/conditions-and-diseases/coronavirus/covid19-and-anxiety.

12   Donald A. Schön, Beyond the Stable State: Public and Private
Learning in a Changing Society (London: Maurice Temple Smith
Ltd., 1971).

13   Keith Grint, "Problems, Problems, Problems: The Social Construction of Leadership," Human Relations 58, no. 11 (2005):
1467–1494.

14   Daniel Grupe and Jack Nitschke, "Uncertainty and Anticipation
in Anxiety: An Integrated Neurobiological and Psychological
Perspective," Nature Reviews Neuroscience 14 (2013): 488–501,
https://doi.org/10.1038/nrn3524.

15   Larry Hirschhorn, The Workplace Within: Psychodynamics of
Organizational Life (Cambridge, MA: MIT Press, 1988) 45.

16   Deirdre Moylan, "Contagion," in The Unconscious at Work: A
Tavistock Approach to Making Sense of Organisational Life, ed.
Anton Obholzer and Vega Zagier Roberts (London/New York:
Routledge, 2019).

17   Larry Hirschhorn, The Workplace Within: Psychodynamics of
Organizational Life (Cambridge, MA: MIT Press, 1988).

18   Melanie Klein, "Notes on Some Schizoid Mechanisms," The
Journal of Psychotherapy Practice and Research 5 (Spring 1946):
160–179.

19   W. H. Auden, The Age of Anxiety (New York: Random House,
1947).

20   William Goldman, All the President's Men, directed by Alan J.
Pakula (Burbank, CA: Warner Bros., 1976), film. Though widely
attributed to the Watergate investigation, the phrase "Follow the
money" was popularised by this film and does not appear in the
original reporting or book by Woodward and Bernstein.

21   Carl Bernstein and Bob Woodward, All the President's Men (New York: Simon & Schuster, 1974), 151.

22   Melanie Klein, "Notes on Some Schizoid Mechanisms," The Journal of Psychotherapy Practice and Research 5 (Spring 1946): 160–179.

23   Ibid.

24   Isabel Menzies Lyth, "Social Systems as a Defence Against Anxiety: An Empirical Study of the Nursing Service of a General Hospital," in Social Engagement of Social Science, Volume 1: The Socio-Psychological Perspective, ed. Eric Trist and Hugh Murray (London: Free Association Books, 1990), 439–462.

25   Rainer Maria Rilke, Letters to a Young Poet (Leipzig: Insel-Verlag, 1929).

26   Daniel Goleman, Emotional Intelligence: Why It Can Matter More Than IQ (London: Bloomsbury Publishing, 1998).

27   Daniel Goleman, Emotional Intelligence: Why It Can Matter More Than IQ (London: Bloomsbury Publishing, 1998), 371.

28   Ronald S. Britton, "The Missing Link: Parental Sexuality in the Oedipus Complex," in The Oedipus Complex Today: Clinical Implications, ed. James Steiner (London: Karnac Books, 1989), 83–101.

29   Ibid.

30   Wilfred Bion. 1961. Experiences in Groups and Other Papers. London: Tavistock Publications.

31   Larry Hirschhorn, The Workplace Within: Psychodynamics of Organizational Life (Cambridge, MA: MIT Press, 1988).

32   Andrew Cooper and Tim Dartington. 2004. "The Vanishing Organisation: Organisational Containment in a Networked World." In Working Below the Surface: The Emotional Life of Contemporary Organisations, edited by Clare Huffington, David Armstrong, William Halton, Linda Hoyle, and Jane Pooley, 127–150. London: Karnac Books.

33   Deirdre Moylan, "Contagion," in The Unconscious at Work: A Tavistock Approach to Making Sense of Organisational Life, ed. Anton Obholzer and Vega Zagier Roberts (London/New York: Routledge, 2019).

34   Larry Hirschhorn, The Workplace Within: Psychodynamics of Organizational Life (Cambridge, MA: MIT Press, 1988).

35   Wilfred R. Bion, Learning from Experience (London/New York: Rowman & Littlefield Publishers, 1962).

36   Donald W. Winnicott. 1953. "Transitional Objects and Transitional Phenomena: A Study of the First Not-Me Possession." International Journal of Psycho-Analysis 34: 89–97.

37   David Armstrong, Organization in the Mind: Psychoanalysis, Group Relations, and Organizational Consultancy (London/New York: Karnac Books, 2005).

38   Ibid.

39   Martin Heidegger, Being and Time (Tübingen: Niemeyer, 1927).

40   Paul Gilbert, The Compassionate Mind (London: Constable, 2013).

41   Wilfred R. Bion, Learning from Experience (London/New York: Rowman & Littlefield Publishers, 1962), 36.

42   Melanie Klein, "Notes on Some Schizoid Mechanisms," The Journal of Psychotherapy Practice and Research 5 (Spring 1946): 160–179.

43   Larry Hirschhorn, Reworking Authority: Leading and Following in the Post-Modern Organization (Cambridge, MA: MIT Press, 1997).

44   Eric Berne, Transactional Analysis in Psychotherapy: The Classic Handbook to Its Principles (London: Condor, 1961).

45   Isabel Menzies Lyth, "Social Systems as a Defence Against Anxiety: An Empirical Study of the Nursing Service of a General Hospital," in Social Engagement of Social Science, Volume 1: The Socio-Psychological Perspective, ed. Eric Trist and Hugh Murray (London: Free Association Books, 1990), 439–462.

46   John F. Kennedy, Profiles in Courage (New York: Harper & Brothers, 1955).

47   Guilaine Kinouani, Living While Black: The Essential Guide to Overcoming Racial Trauma (London: Ebury Press, 2021).

48   Peter Simpson, Robert French, and Carol Harvey, "Leadership and Negative Capability," Human Relations 55, no. 10 (2002): 1209–1226.

49   Aileen Ward. 1963. John Keats: The Making of a Poet. New York: Viking Press.

50   Kenneth Eisold, "The Rediscovery of the Unknown: An Inquiry into Psychoanalytic Praxis," Contemporary Psychoanalysis 36, no. 1 (2000): 57–75, https://doi.org/10.1080/00107530.2000.107470 45.

51   Ronald Heifetz, Marty Linsky, and Alexander Grashow, The Practice of Adaptive Leadership: Tools and Tactics for Changing Your Organization and the World (Boston: Harvard Business Press, 2009).

52   A. K. Rice, Learning for Leadership: Interpersonal and Inter-group Relations (London: Tavistock Publications, 1965).

53   Ronald Heifetz, Marty Linsky, and Alexander Grashow, The Practice of Adaptive Leadership: Tools and Tactics for Changing Your Organization and the World (Boston: Harvard Business Press, 2009).

54   Ronald S. Britton, "The Missing Link: Parental Sexuality in the Oedipus Complex," in The Oedipus Complex Today: Clinical Implications, ed. James Steiner (London: Karnac Books, 1989), 83–101.

55   Ronald Heifetz, Marty Linsky, and Alexander Grashow, The Practice of Adaptive Leadership: Tools and Tactics for Changing Your Organization and the World (Boston: Harvard Business Press, 2009).

56   Ibid.

57   Søren Kierkegaard, The Concept of Anxiety (Copenhagen: Reitzel, 1844).

58   Eric Berne, Transactional Analysis in Psychotherapy: The Classic Handbook to Its Principles (London: Condor, 1961).

59   James Hollis, Finding Meaning in the Second Half of Life, 2005

60   Beverley Taylor, Reflective Practice: A Guide for Nurses and Midwives (UK: Allen and Unwin; Melbourne: Open University Press, 2000).

61   Ronald Heifetz, Marty Linsky, and Alexander Grashow, The Practice of Adaptive Leadership: Tools and Tactics for Changing Your Organization and the World (Boston: Harvard Business Press, 2009)..

62   Carl Gustav Jung, Collected Works of C.G. Jung (London: Routledge & Kegan Paul, 1953).

63   Ronald S. Britton, "The Missing Link: Parental Sexuality in the Oedipus Complex," in The Oedipus Complex Today: Clinical Implications, ed. James Steiner (London: Karnac Books, 1989), 83–101.

64   Red Hawk, Self-Observation: The Awakening of Conscience: An Owner's Manual (Arizona: Hohm Press, 2009).

65   Ibid.

66   Sigmund Freud, "Recommendations to Physicians Practising Psycho-Analysis," in The Standard Edition of the Complete Psychological Works of Sigmund Freud, vol. XII (1911–1913): The Case of Schreber, Papers on Technique and Other Works, 111–120 (London: Hogarth Press, 1912).

67   Ronald S. Britton, "The Missing Link: Parental Sexuality in the Oedipus Complex," in The Oedipus Complex Today: Clinical Implications, ed. James Steiner (London: Karnac Books, 1989), 83–101.

68   Carl Gustav Jung, Collected Works of C.G. Jung (London: Routledge & Kegan Paul, 1953).

69   Maurice Nicoll, Psychological Commentaries on the Teaching of Gurdjieff and Ouspensky (London: Vincent Stuart Publishers, 1980).

70   Red Hawk, Self-Observation: The Awakening of Conscience: An Owner's Manual (Arizona: Hohm Press, 2009).

71   John O'Donohue, Anam Cara: A Book of Celtic Wisdom (London: Bantam Books, 1997).

72   Red Hawk, Self-Observation: The Awakening of Conscience: An Owner's Manual (Arizona: Hohm Press, 2009).

73   Ibid.

74   Wilfred R. Bion, Learning from Experience (London/New York: Rowman & Littlefield Publishers, 1962).

75   Melanie Klein, "Notes on Some Schizoid Mechanisms," The Journal of Psychotherapy Practice and Research 5 (Spring 1946): 160–179.

76   Ibid.

77   John O'Donohue, Anam Cara: A Book of Celtic Wisdom (London: Bantam Books, 1997).

78   C. G. Jung, Modern Man in Search of a Soul, trans. W. S. Dell and Cary F. Baynes (London: Routledge & Kegan Paul, 1933), 234.

79   Carl Gustav Jung, Collected Works of C.G. Jung (London: Routledge & Kegan Paul, 1953).

80   Rumi, The Essential Rumi, trans. Coleman Barks (New York: HarperOne, 2004).

81   Ibid.

82   Paul Tillich, The Courage to Be, 2nd ed. (New Haven: Yale University Press, 2000; first published 1952).

83   Melanie Klein, "Notes on Some Schizoid Mechanisms," The Journal of Psychotherapy Practice and Research 5 (Spring 1946): 160–179.

84   Ibid.

85   Rumi, The Essential Rumi, trans. Coleman Barks (New York: HarperOne, 2004).

Index